WEXNER CENTER FOR THE VISUAL ARTS, THE OHIO STATE UNIVERSITY

WEXNER CENTER FOR THE VISUAL ARTS, THE OHIO STATE UNIVERSITY

A building designed by Eisenman/Trott Architects, with critical essays by Rafael Moneo and Anthony Vidler, and introductions by Dr. Edward H. Jennings, President, The Ohio State University; Leslie H. Wexner, Chairman of the Board, the Limited; Robert Stearns, Director of the Wexner Center for the Visual Arts; and Jonathan Green, Founding Project Director, Wexner Center for the Visual Arts.

Part 1: Texts
Dr. Edward H. Jennings
Comments, 20
Leslie H. Wexner
Comments, 23
Robert Stearns
Building as Catalyst, 24
Jonathan Green
Algorithms for Discovery, 28
Anthony Vidler
Counter-Monuments in Practice: The Wexner Center for the Visual Arts, 32
Rafael Moneo
Unexpected Coincidences, 40

Part 2: Design and Concept, 48
Part 3: Construction, 102
Part 4: The Building, 154

RIZZOLI
NEW YORK

First published in the United States of America
1989 by
RIZZOLI INTERNATIONAL
PUBLICATIONS, INC.
300 Park Avenue South, New York, NY 10010

Copyright © 1989 Rizzoli International
Publications, Inc.
All rights reserved.
No part of this publication may be reproduced
in any manner whatsoever without permission
in writing from Rizzoli International
Publications, Inc.
Library of Congress Catalog Card Number
89-45421
ISBN 0-8478-1116-6 (paperback)
ISBN 0-8478-1115-8 (hardcover)
This project was made possible through the
generous support of The Ohio State University.

Designer: Massimo Vignelli
Design Coordinator: Judy Geib
Assistants: Sabine Buell, John Durschinger
Editorial Assistance: Henry Urbach
Set in type by Strong Silent Type, New York
Printed and bound in Japan
Sketches by Peter Eisenman, courtesy Max
Protetch Gallery.

PHOTOGRAPHY

Part 1: Photograph of newspaper clippings by
Dick Frank Studio; photograph of the
competition model, courtesy The Ohio State
University; photographs of Robert Stearns,
Claudia Gould, and Jim Rudy, and Sarah
Rogers-Lafferty and William Horrigan on the
construction site © Jeff Goldberg/ESTO;
photo of Progressive Architecture Award
Ceremony, l. to r. Peter Eisenman, Jonathan
Green, Richard Trott, James Murphy, by
Darlene Studios, New York; Peter Eisenman
and Richard Trott on the site photographed by
Louie Psihoyos, MATRIX; photograph of the
OSU stadium with the band spelling "Ohio" in
script, by V. Scott Gilford.
Part 2: Aerial photo, courtesy The Ohio State
University; photo-collages and competition
model, Dick Frank Studio; final model,
Wolfgang Hoyt.
Part 3: James Friedman. The construction of
the Wexner Center was documented for The
Ohio State University in 8x10 color negatives,
which are reproduced here in black and white.
Part 4: © Jeff Goldberg/ESTO

BUILDING CREDITS

Client: The Ohio State University, Columbus, Ohio; James Swiatek, University Project Architect; Tom Heretta, University Project Manager

Architect:
Eisenman/Trott Architects, Inc., New York and Columbus, Ohio
Partners-in-Charge: Peter Eisenman, Richard Trott
Directing Architects: Michael Burkey, George Kewin
Project Architects: Arthur Baker, Andrew Buchsbaum, Thomas Leeser, Richard Morris, James Rudy, Faruk Yorgancioglu
Project Team: Andrea Brown, Edward Carroll, Robert Choeff, David Clark, Chuck Crawford, Tim Decker, Ellen Dunham, Frances Hsu, Wes Jones, Jim Linke, Michael McInturf, Hiroshi Maruyama, Mark Mascheroni, Alexis Moser, Harry Ours, Joe Rosa, Scott Sickeler, Madison Spencer, Mark Wamble.

Consultants:
Landscape Architect:
Hanna/Olin, Ltd., Philadelphia; Laurie Olin, Partner-in-Charge
Structural Engineer:
Lantz, Jones, & Nebraska, Inc.; Tom Jones, Partner-in-Charge
Mechanical Engineer: H.A. Williams & Associates
Lighting Design: Jules Fisher & Paul Marantz, Inc.
Civil Engineer: C.F. Bird & P.J. Bull, Ltd.
Security and Fire: Joseph M. Chapman, Inc.
Graphics and Color: Robert Slutzky
Soils Engineer: Dunbar Geotechnical
AudioVisual: Boyce Nemec
Specifications: George Van Neil
Models: Albert Maloof, Gen Servini, Scale Images
Renderings: Brian Burr
Model Photography: Dick Frank, Wolfgang Hoyt
Construction Photographs: James Friedman, Will Shively and D.G. Olshavsky/ARTOG
Final Photographs: Jeff Goldberg/ESTO and D.G. Olshavsky/ARTOG

Contractors:

Dugan and Meyers, General Contractor
Jim Smith, Project Manager;
A.T.F. Mechanical, Inc., Mechanical Contractor,
Bob Weiland, Project Manager;
Romanoff Electric, Electrical Contractor
Sib Goelz, Project Superintendent;
Radico, Inc., Plumbing Contractor
Frank Czako, Project Manager;
J.T. Edwards, Steel Subcontractor
Jack Edwards, President

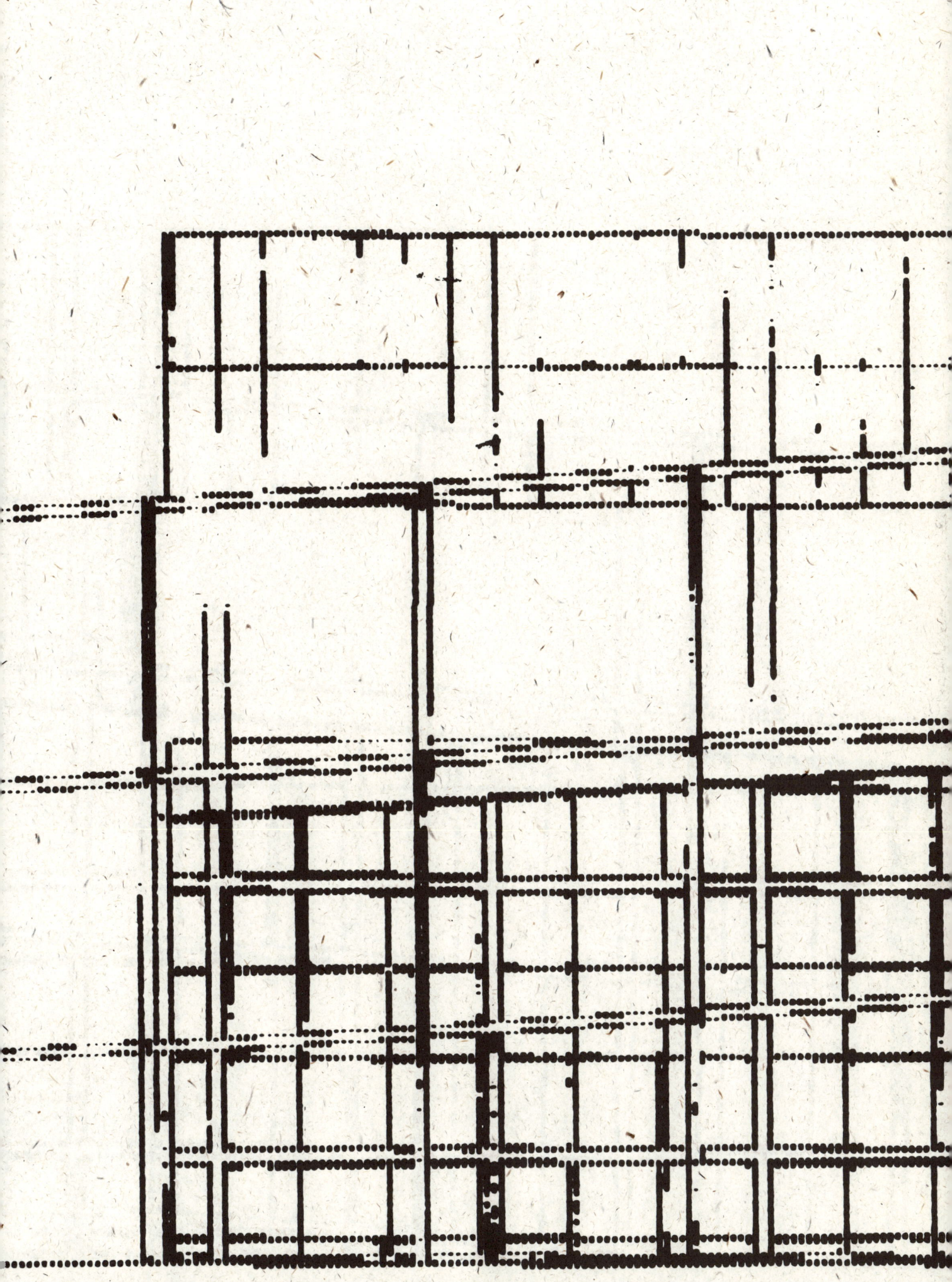

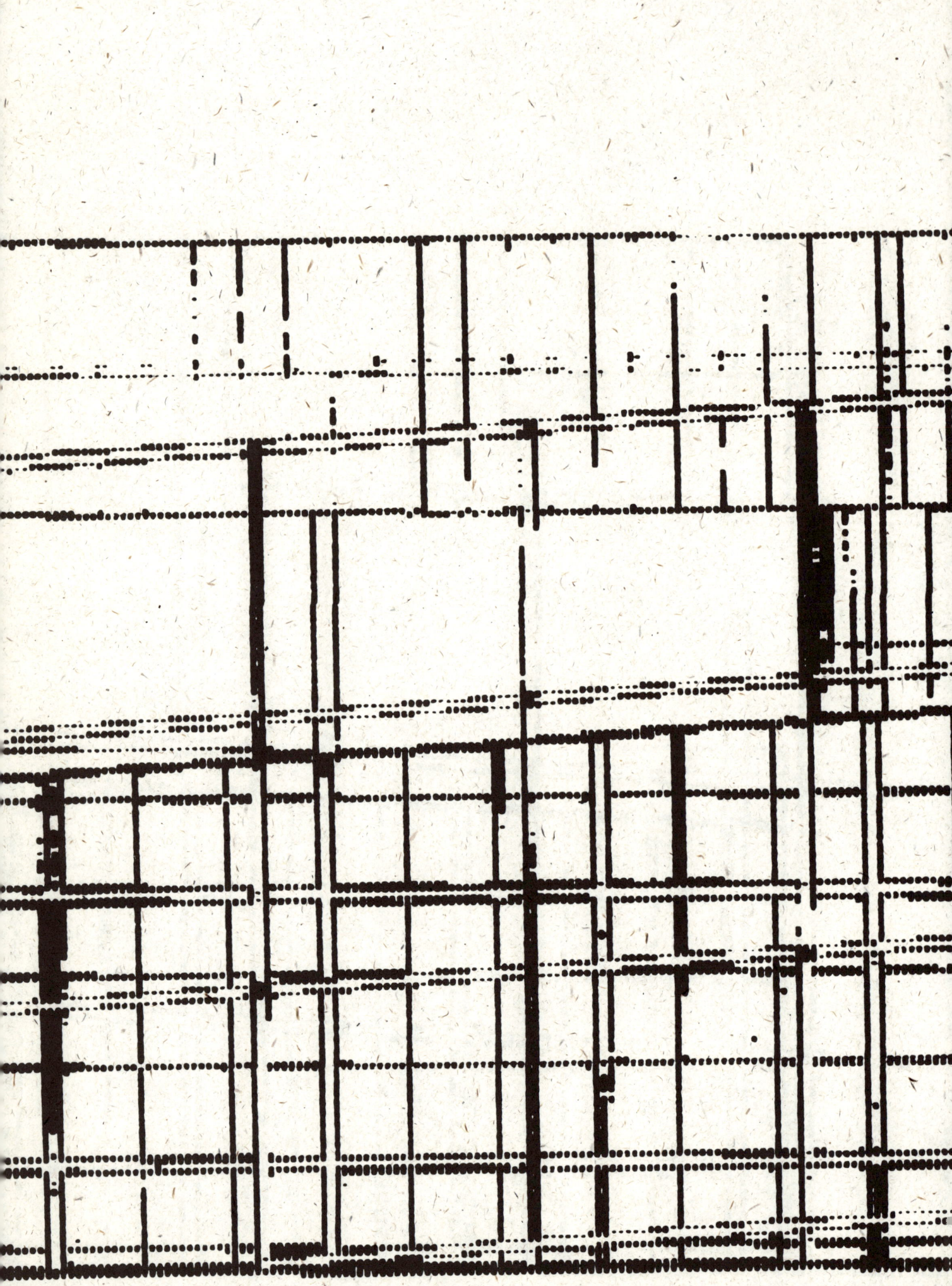

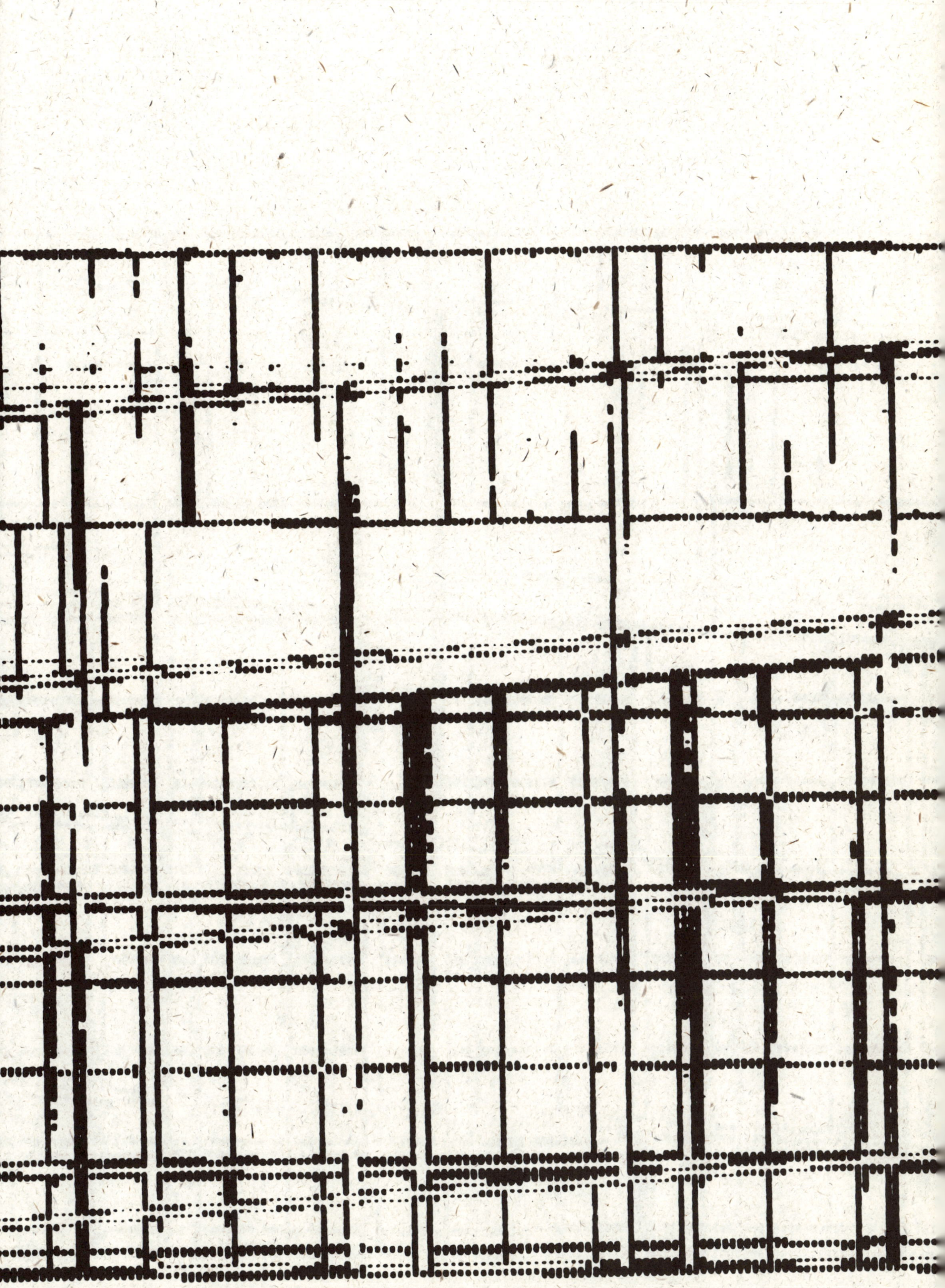

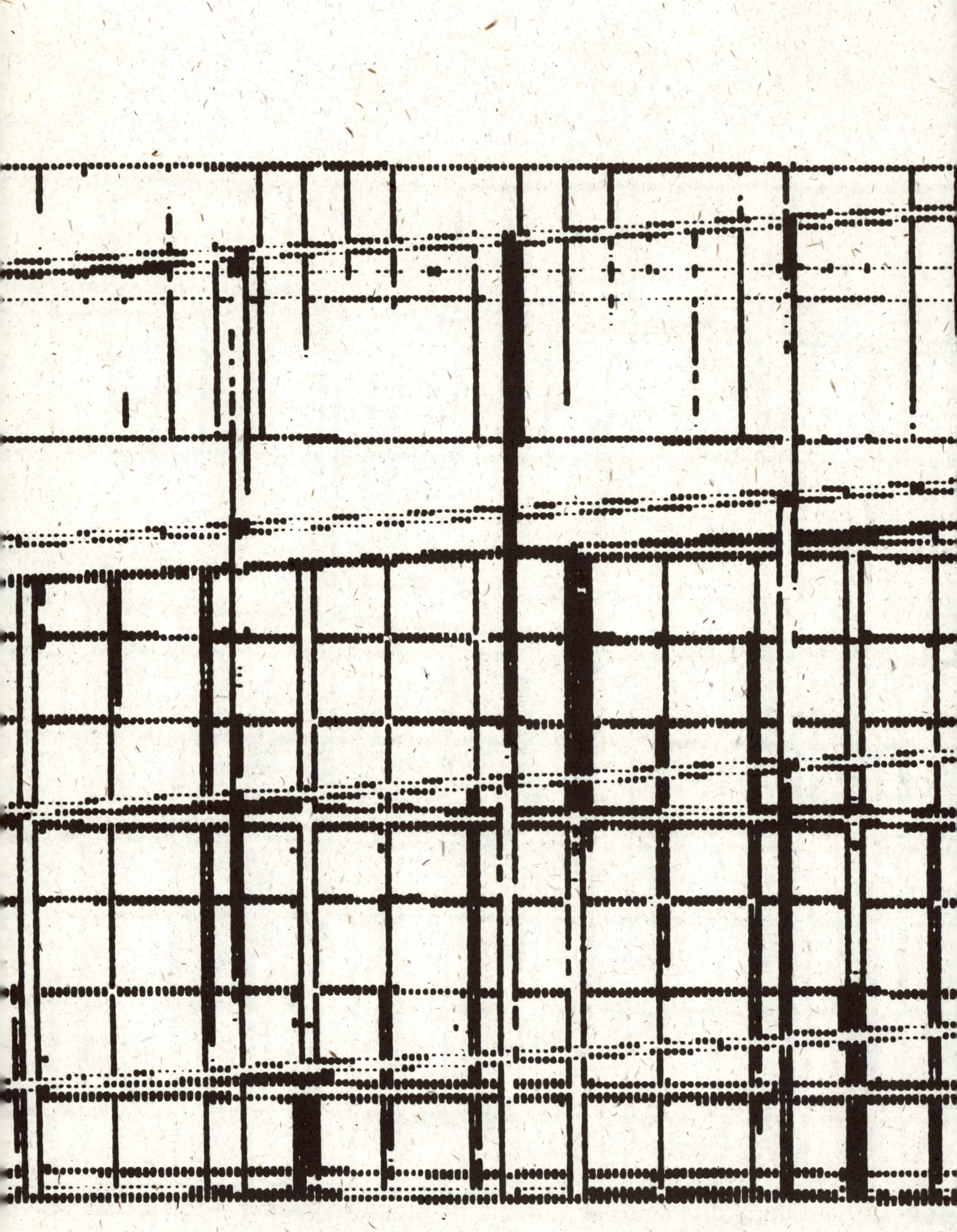

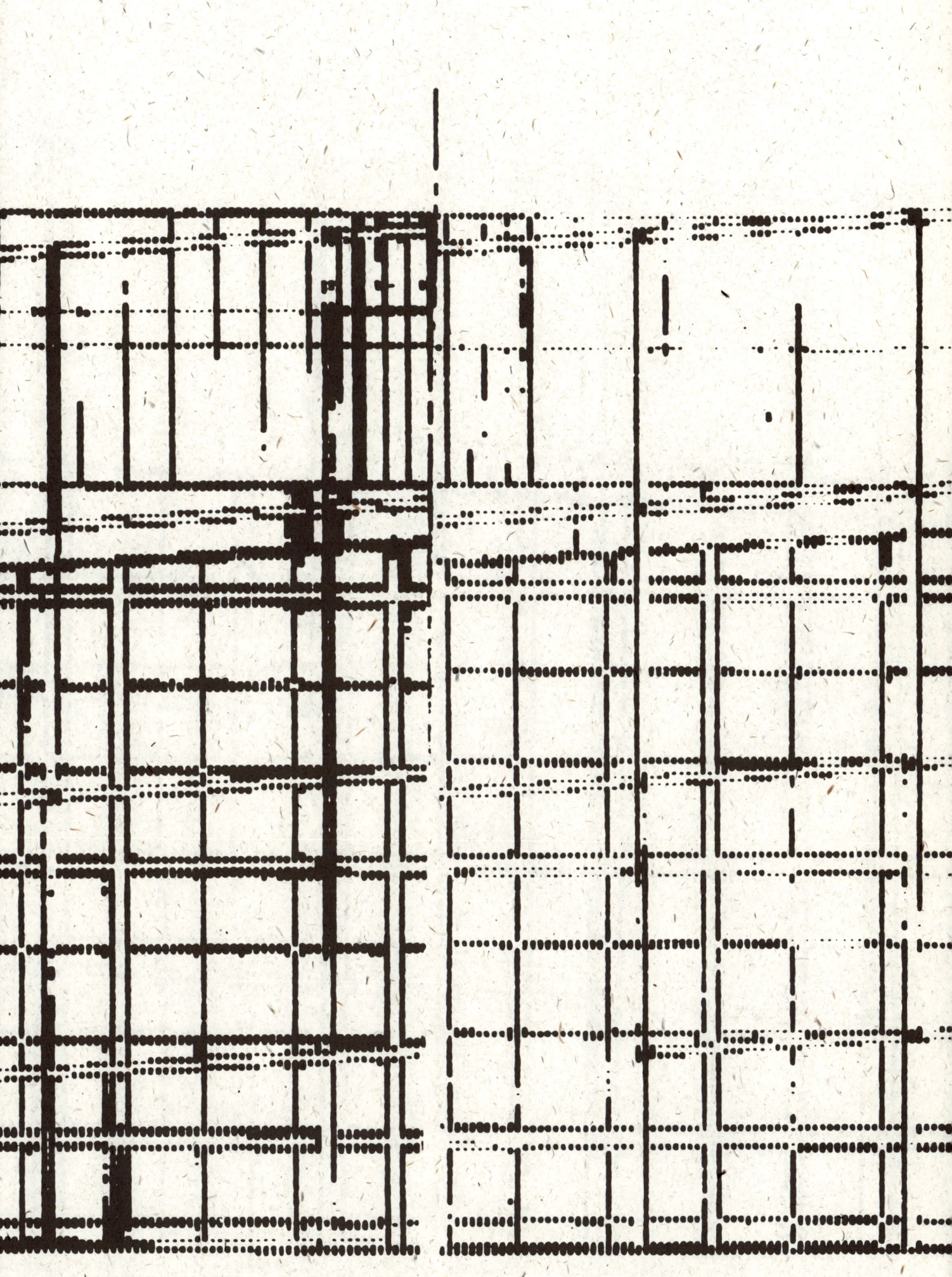

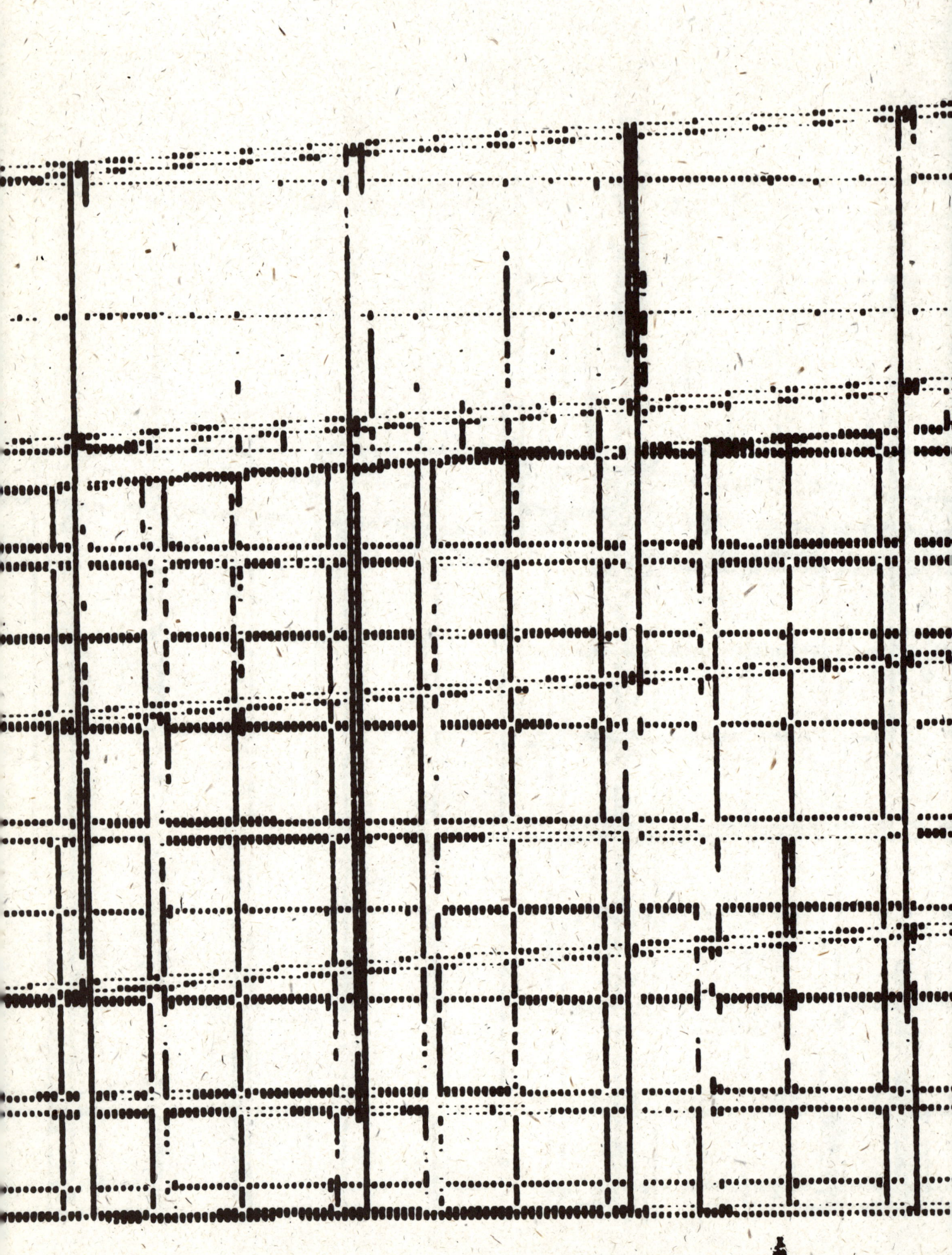

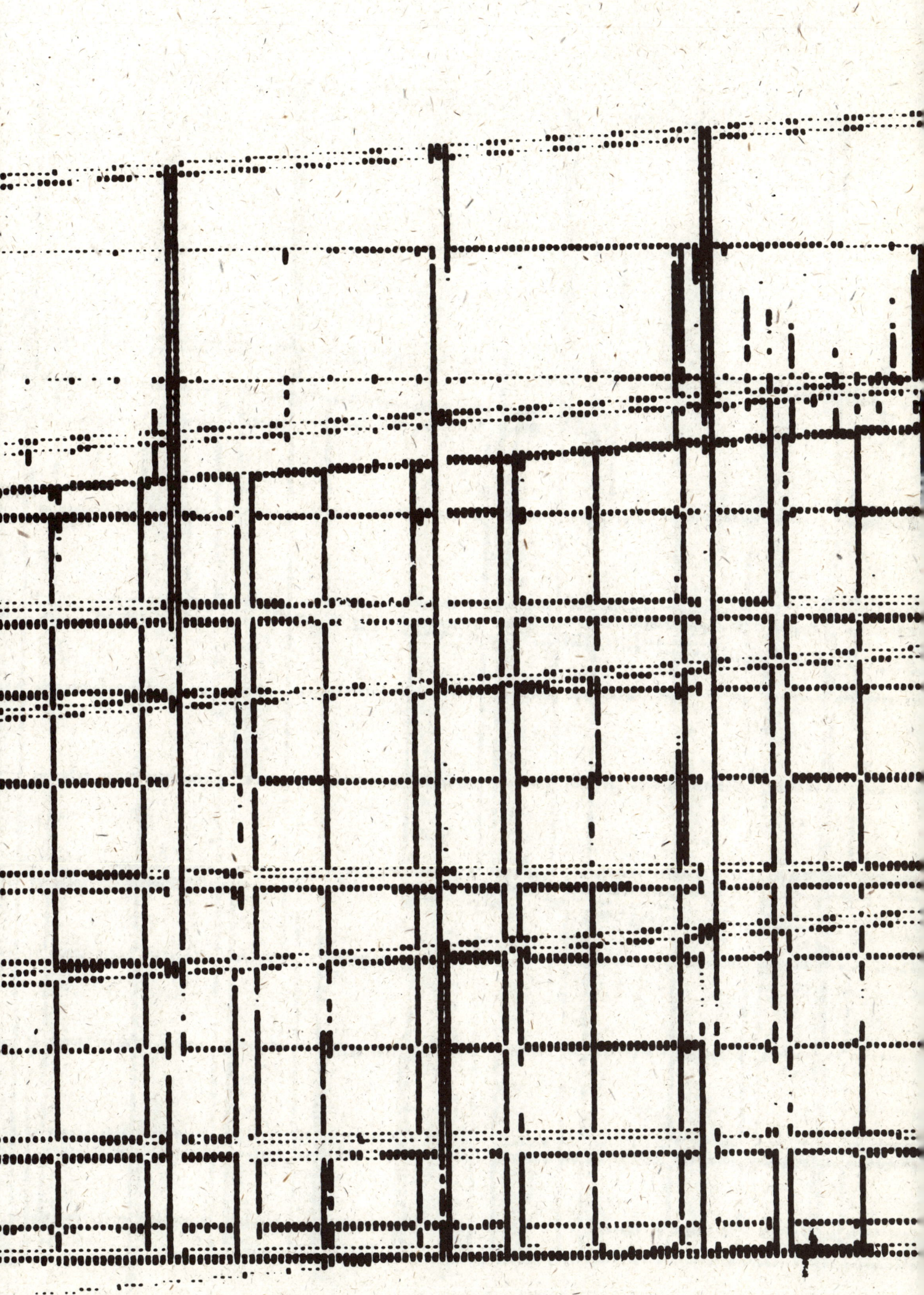

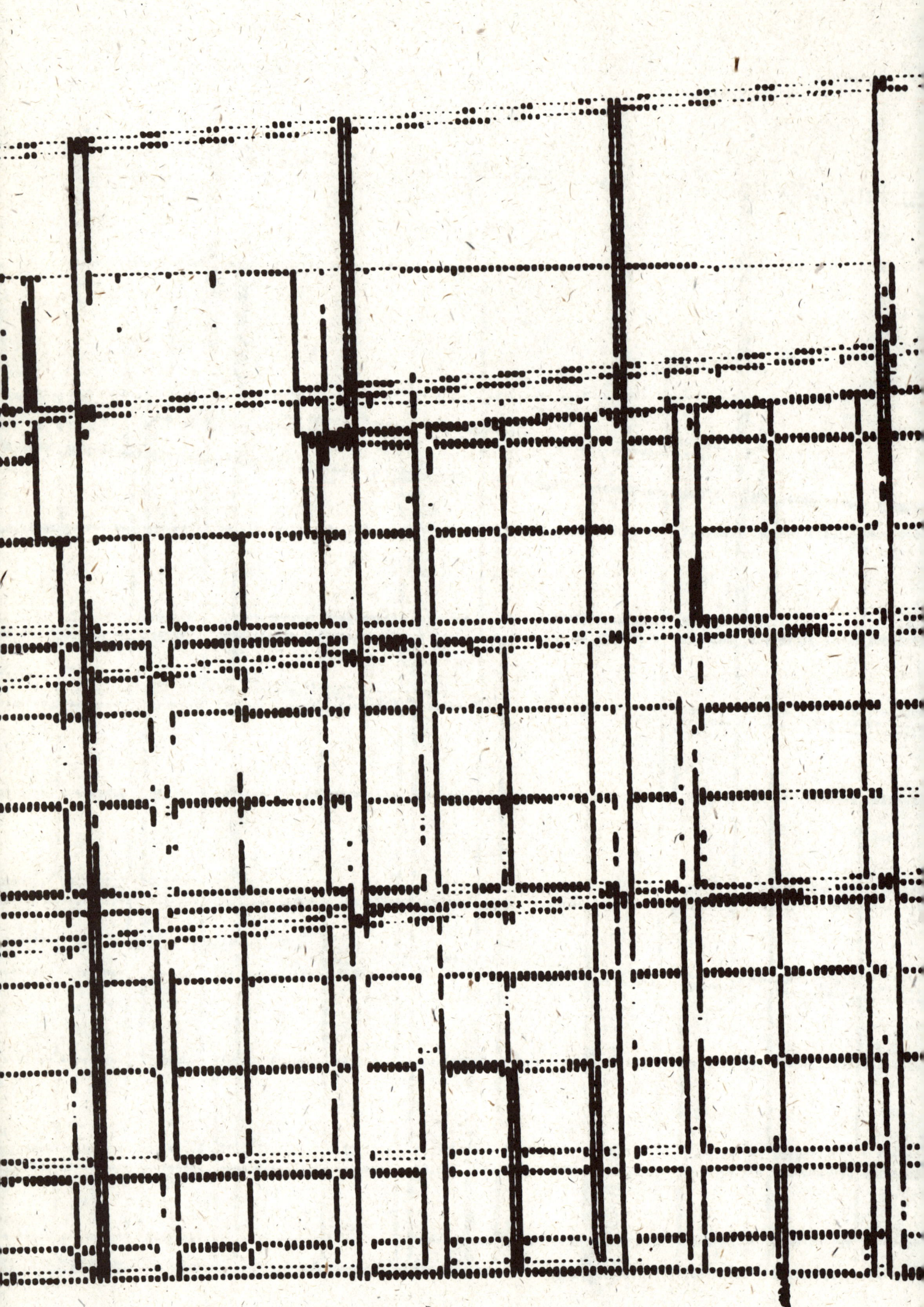

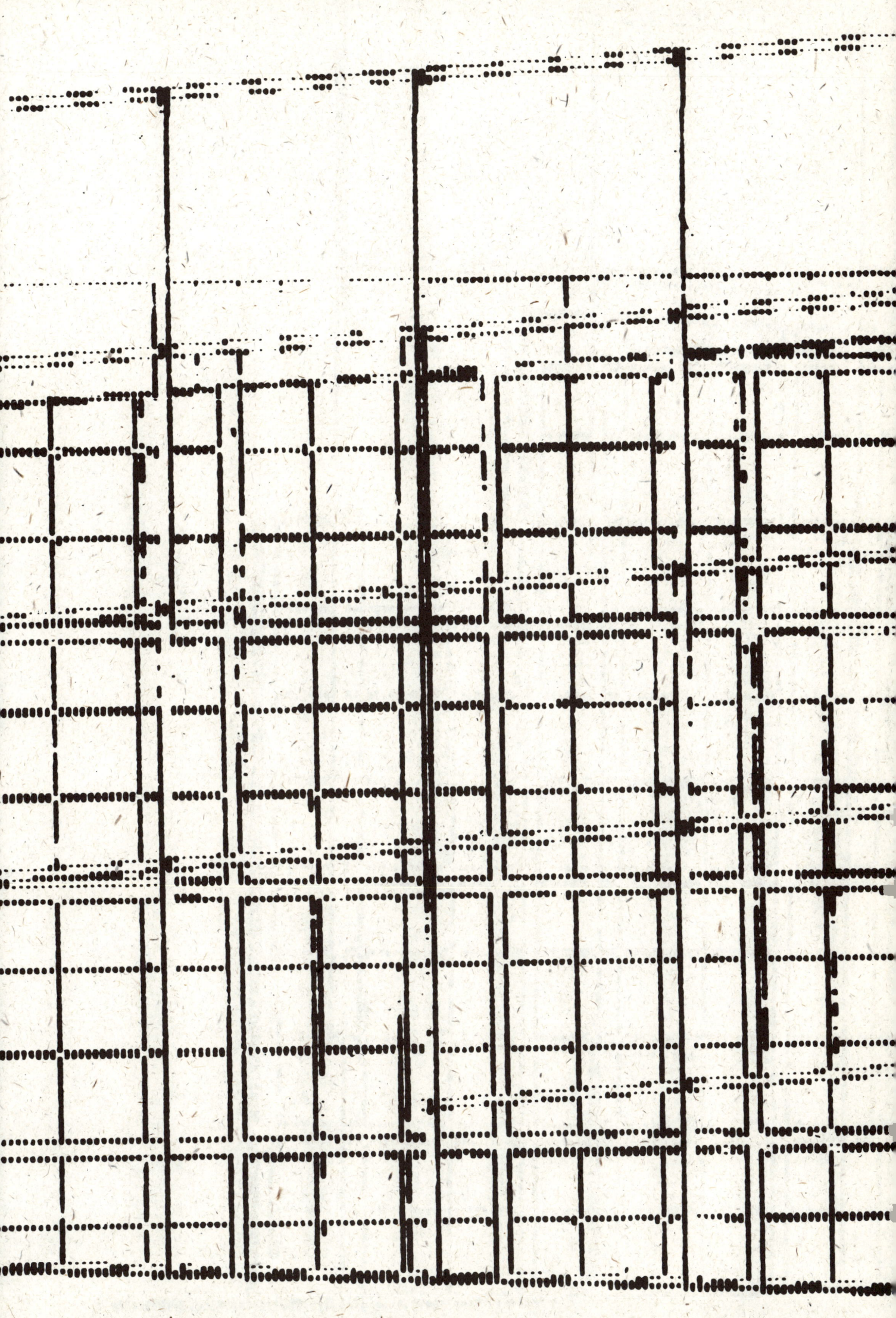

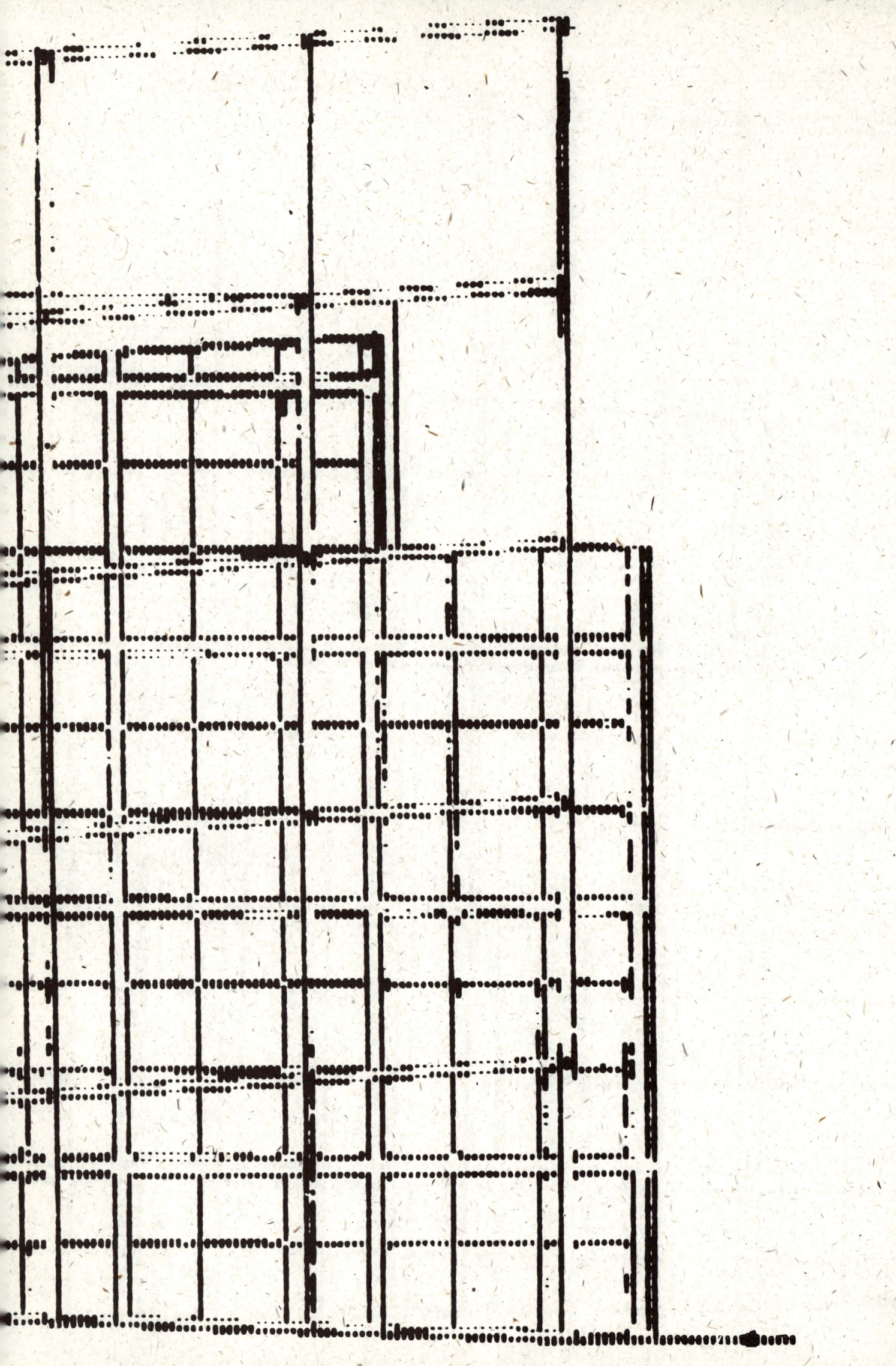

PRESIDENT'S COMMENTS
Dr. Edward H. Jennings

The Ohio State University has a special role as Ohio's land-grant university and fulfills a three-part mission defined by its heritage: teaching, research, and related service. The Wexner Center for the Visual Arts will, through its extraordinary facilities and outstanding programs, enhance the excellence of Ohio State in many ways.

As a land-grant institution, the University is committed to providing an educational opportunity to all qualified individuals, independent of their social standing, gender, or financial need. Thus, Ohio State boasts great diversity among its students, faculty, and staff members. This enriches the educational environment for all who live, work, and study here.

Like its students and faculty, Ohio State's curriculum is truly international in scope. Cross-cultural perspectives are critical to achieving our educational goals. Furthermore, within the curriculum of the land-grant universities is the integration of liberal education with professional preparation so that our graduates are educated, creative, and adaptable to the future.

The responsibility for basic research should be assigned primarily to universities. Through interdisciplinary collaborations, facilitated by Ohio State's comprehensive nature, and through the creativity and energy of students and faculty working together, Ohio State has emerged as a great research university.

A further outgrowth of the land-grant act was the concept of service as it related to teaching and research. We are charged to move our research results to the practical arena so that they can be rapidly and fully exploited by the community at large.

The Wexner Center for the Visual Arts plays a significant role in our three-fold mission. This remarkable facility of award-winning design is a pathway to the University, linking the community and our Columbus campus. By its prominent location, it clearly communicates the central role that the arts play in our educational environment.

Ohio State's fifth president, William Oxley Thompson, remarked in 1924 that "liberal education is more often caught than taught." There is much truth in this statement; all of us are aware of how much we learned beyond the classroom, the laboratory, and the studio. The presence of the Wexner Center, by its remarkable design, its location, and by the excellence of the programs it will house, will engage all who pass by in a way that truly reflects the institution's core values of creativity, exploration, and free expression.

An intellectual community cannot be complete without attention to the abiding value and influence of the Fine Arts. The Ohio State University recognizes the critical role of the arts in a great University and in a community of educated women and men. Our commitment to create a visual arts center for the campus exemplifies a specific field in which excellence cannot fail to enhance the institution as a whole.

The Wexner Center provides a home for Ohio State's significant holdings of art objects. More importantly, it provides an environment in which students, scholars, artists, designers, and the larger community can work, study, create, explore, and enjoy some of the world's finest work. It truly integrates our missions and represents the highest standards toward which we strive.

The generosity of Leslie H. Wexner, which has made this Center possible, reflects his commitment to the arts and to enriching the quality of his alma mater. The Ohio State University is deeply grateful to him and to the thousands of friends of this University whose support provides a margin of excellence for one of this nation's truly great universities.

COMMENTS
Leslie H. Wexner

While the roots of a Center for the Arts at The Ohio State University go back more than a decade, this new facility is intended to begin a new and unprecedented chapter in the arts in a university setting.

Although it will house The Ohio State University's art collection, provide four galleries for exhibition and two public presentation spaces, the Center is designed to be more than the sum of its parts. Bringing all of the traditional arts together with the new visual technologies under one roof and joining them in dynamic dialogue with outstanding visiting artists, scholars and critics will create a living workshop for the arts. To design a building to accommodate this dynamic program was the challenge faced by the Center's architects, Richard Trott and Peter Eisenman. That they have more than successfully met this challenge is evident to all who will visit and use this state-of-the-art facility.

The next challenge, however, lies in the future, in fulfilling the vision of integrating teaching, research and exhibition at a level of excellence to match the building's striking and exciting architectural design. If this architectural tour de force succeeds in invigorating The Ohio State University and the community to a new standard of excellence in the arts; if it serves as a magnet for attracting outstanding faculty, artists and students, and is a showcase for the best of today's art and artists, then it will achieve its real purpose.

The Wexner Center for the Arts, both in its program and architecture, is intended to set a new standard of what a university can and must do as it seeks to be a catalyst for excellence and innovation in the arts and a model for others to follow.

It is this great vision that stimulated and inspired all those involved to take this step into the future of the arts and architecture. Many minds and talents have joined forces to bring a center for the arts at The Ohio State University into reality. A new visual landmark has been created on the University campus and with it, The Ohio State University has made a commitment to be at the vanguard of creativity in the visual arts and a world center for artistic collaboration.

BUILDING AS CATALYST
Robert Stearns

The Wexner Center for the Visual Arts opens in a charged atmosphere of unprecedented construction of houses of culture around the world. New buildings, renovations and museum additions in the past ten years have served as fertile testing grounds for applying the art of architecture to the presentation of the arts. The results are providing a provocative array of structures which have generated world-wide debate on the degree of their success in providing for the needs of artists, curators and their audiences.

Within this energized landscape, the Wexner Center for the Visual Arts emerges, potentially, as a unique institution. There is no question this building raises questions. Its design and its program are intended to. While the Center will "collect, preserve and interpret works of art," it will present and challenge all forms of the contemporary arts and encourage the creation of new works and new technologies in the service of art. Situated within a major research university, the Center is, most importantly, about investigation and exploration in the arts. In some senses, its programs will be similar to other institutions, devoting its resources to exposing recent developments in painting and sculpture, architecture, the graphic and design arts, the performing arts of dance, theater and music and the media arts of film, video and sound. Education programs will make the arts, in all these forms, accessible to a broad public. But, the similarity to other institutions ends here.

This program will be housed within a new facility which challenges conventional thinking in museum design and programming, whether traditional or contemporary. As the fine nuances or bold gestures of other new museum designs are discussed by critics of the field, the emergence of the Wexner Center for the Visual Arts will likely derail polite conversation on the topic. The Eisenman/Trott design provides unresolved, open-ended questions awaiting response and interaction by artists, curators and audiences. It demands innovative approaches to exhibitions and to the performance-related arts, and by doing that, the building itself begs a critical review of the role and function of museums in today's society.

Eisenman and Trott were charged with designing a center to present "art of the twenty-first century," meaning art that does not yet exist. But, as early twentieth century utopian visions of an ordered future have dissolved into chaos, the result here is not, and could not have been, a Bauhaus-style remake. Instead, like art today (and in the future?), the building is eclectic and multi-layered. It thrives on dichotomies. It is airy yet dense; grand but intimate. While the new construction comprises almost 130,000 square feet, it is more of an event than a building. Oddly self-effacing in its low profile, it thrusts out from behind the surrounding, existing structures of Mershon Auditorium and Weigel Hall. It is nonetheless aggressive; massive brick towers evolve into a filigree of white scaffold tracery. Inside, the invasive grids and axes project themselves into spaces and onto walls and floors creating a multi-rhythmic polyphony as one logic system collides with another. The structure and design have emerged from conceptual and philosophical issues rather than from presumptions of the function of museums. The charge to integrate the site into its surroundings was addressed through historical references and a grid structure resulting from the overlay of university and community mapping strategies. But, if this design is to amount to more than an accumulation of columns, beams, soffits and a myriad of mullion joints, it will be because the whole presents a nourishing challenge to those who use it, affecting the very nature of what is presented and what comes into being because of it.

Most museums of the past century and a half have called upon previous museum architecture for their legitimacy. From the British Museum, built in the 1820's, to the high neoclassical style of the Brooklyn Museum, designed by McKim, Mead and White in 1893, these structures of the nineteenth century firmly established the posture for art museums and identified them as elevated temples of humanism. An important shift occurred with the Stone and Goodwin design for the original Museum of Modern Art which set the tone for

new twentieth century thinking about galleries for modern art as "neutral" frames conducive to exhibitions of art works that set themselves apart from everything that came before. Reflections and refinements on that notion have included, among many, the "Knox" wing of the Albright Gallery in Buffalo by Gordon Bunshaft, and the Walker Art Center and Dallas Museum of Art, both by Edward Larrabee Barnes. Tangents to this mainstream direction have included Frank Lloyd Wright's helical Guggenheim Museum, Bruce Goff's more recent Oriental ode-to-Terpsichore of the Japanese pavilion at the Los Angeles County Museum and Frank Gehry's California Air and Space Museum. In all these cases, the design is predicated on the central requirement of housing permanent collections and traveling exhibitions that support the premise of those collections. Their historical focus has usually determined the appropriate style of the museum.

Since the mission of the Wexner Center is to challenge even modern conventions and to explore unresolved territories in the arts and to serve as a catalyst for new thinking, this building's form sets that tone immediately by making it impractical—if not impossible—to fall into the comfort zone of familiar solutions. The multi-disciplinary mission of the center is reinforced by its physical make-up, comprising four principal gallery spaces equipped for sound and video and a number of auxiliary exhibition spaces that invite creative uses. These galleries, however, claim little more than ten percent of the overall project. Joining this, in the entire complex, is a two-hundred-and-eighty seat film and video theatre, a "black box" performance space with flexible seating, a *laboratory for the creation of video and audio works, the University's libraries for the fine arts and communications arts, a cafe and bookstore plus support spaces for education studios, art storage, exhibition preparation and administration. This new construction is situated between and unites existing spaces of the three-thousand seat Mershon Auditorium and the seven-hundred-and-twenty seat Weigel Hall, in total comprising almost a quarter million square feet, occupying two city blocks.*

To inaugurate programs in this unconventional structure, the Wexner Center staff is preparing a year-long series of exhibitions, performing and media arts events and educational programs designed to review the legacy of revolutionary thinking in the arts of the recent past and the present. These programs will underscore the continuous thread of visionary achievements produced since World War II—one of the most fertile periods of artistic exploration. Each participating artist in these programs has contributed to essential changes in our perception of the form and content of art. These works have exerted influence on more recent artistic directions, or they may do so on future developments. These programs are intended to lay a foundation for the Center's future.

Artists and specialists participating in Wexner Center programs will include emerging and established talents from the international, national, regional, metropolitan and university communities. Our focus will be on creative artists, critics and researchers whose efforts bring new ideas and works into being: visual artists, choreographers, performance artists, writers and thinkers, composers, playwrights, photographers, etc.

As a contemporary arts center, the Wexner sees its role as a complement to many modern art museums throughout the world but especially to the growing number of multi-disciplinary arts centers including Walker Art Center in Minneapolis, the Museum of Contemporary Art in Los Angeles and, in some ways, the Centre Georges Pompidou in Paris. These centers were founded or have evolved on the premise that the arts of the twentieth century are interdependent and symbiotic. These centers have reasoned that one facility, rather than many, might present to the public a more complete picture of the evolving forms of the arts. For more than twenty years, Walker Art Center has presented film and video works, commissioned new dance and music works and spawned a television series exploring new developments in video and the media arts which continues, now independently. MOCA, too, presents performance works and has created a nationally distributed radio program surveying new directions for art on the air. L'Institut de Recherche et Coordination Acoustique/Musique (IRCAM) is closely associated with the Centre Pompidou and, as an electronic and computer music laboratory, expands the Centre's function as both a modern art museum and cultural information center.

The Wexner Center sees itself as part of another international community, too. Beyond its function as a repository and presenter of art works, the Wexner Center will be a participant in the art-making process. Artists' colonies and similar residency programs offer artists from many disciplines time away from daily duties to explore new ideas. Some have created programs to present completed works or works-in-progress to the public like the Splash Festival of dance at Jacob's Pillow in the Berkshire Mountains. The Brooklyn Academy of Music's Next Wave Festival is perhaps the world's most aggressive promoter of newly commissioned works which meld dance, music, theater and the visual arts. What binds together these and many other efforts is their common goal of providing resources to artists to create new work, to be catalysts in the artistic process.

Joining The Ohio State University's advanced research programs in computer studies, engineering, cancer research, astronomy and many other fields, the Wexner Center adds the component of research in the arts. Through the Center's envisioned Institute for Advanced Activities in the Arts, a program of short and long-term residencies will provide opportunities to artists to expand on previous work and move in new directions, much as these other institutions do. But, the educational environment of the University adds the important element of exchange between the visiting and community artists and among faculty, students and staff which can significantly broaden the impact of such activity through exposure and interaction.

So, the design and structure of the building, which take few if any cues from the past, suggest a new and different future for the arts and art centers. The traditional museum context for art as a passive object in a hermetic setting is not here. This building will drive a program of engagement between artist and curator, between artists and viewers and between artists and architecture. This building is a catalyst for many forces active in the creative process.

The building of the Wexner Center and its program has and will require a great deal of effort. President Edward Jennings and Provost Myles Brand have expressed the University's commitment and vision for the Wexner Center's role in the University. Leslie Wexner's financial commitment has made the facilities a reality. Dean Emeritus Andrew Broekema and Founding Project Director Jonathan Green have forged important conceptual groundwork. College of the Arts Dean Donald Harris has articulated the artistic challenges for the College. They, with the faculty and administrative staff of the University and, most of all, the staff of the Wexner Center, will be the team to infuse this Center with life as we move ahead in the years to come.

ALGORITHMS FOR DISCOVERY
Jonathan Green

In classical modernist galleries, as in churches, one does not speak in a normal voice; one does not laugh, eat, drink, lie down, or sleep; one does not get ill, go mad, sing, dance, or make love.
Thomas McEvilley, Introduction to Brian O'Doherty's Inside the White Cube, 1976.

1. Seven and one half years ago, in the spring of 1982, the University Gallery of Fine Arts, expanding upon a program initiated by the Gallery's first director, Betty Collings, and encouraged by Dean Andrew Broekema and a host of faculty within the College of the Arts, proposed to President Edward Jennings a Center for the Visual Arts. This project has now come to fruition with the opening of a challenging new building. From the beginning, Peter Eisenman and Richard Trott's proposal was aesthetically and philosophically consonant with the Center's proposed program. The building owes much of its success to the explicit set of requirements given to the architects and to the ongoing dialogue between university and architect. But the parallels between the architectural solutions and the program stem from a more fundamental congruence than could be derived through document or dialogue.

Thomas McEvilley's enumeration of disallowed gallery activities provides a wry but accurate representation of the concept that underwrites both the architecture and the program for the Center. Where a traditional building would isolate the viewer in a neutral museum space, protecting and insulating him from the realities and processes of the world, the Center's intentions were radical exploration, confrontation, incorporation and inclusion. Both the intentions of the program and the architecture lay beyond the bounds of the traditional disciplines of art and architecture and beyond the limits of traditional design strategy and museum practice. The architecture for the Center, like its program, is a reflection of the most persuasive artistic and critical practice at the end of the twentieth century: a postmodern practice and criticism that has re-evaluated and re-assessed the validity of the modern experiment and has tempered the modernist absolutist persuasion with a relativism and a respect for the context and embedded meaning of the work of art. Both program and architecture are anchored in a belief that the ultimate concerns of art and expression lie in the social domains of economics, politics, and history rather than in the narrowly defined records of aesthetics and styles rehearsed in art or architectural texts. Both share a commitment to the cross referencing of ideas and the re-examination of historical work in new contexts. Both feel an obligation to analyze and understand the social function of art and its relationship to the world of social responsibilities and institutions.

Both architecture and program believe in the generative potential of process itself. From the beginning both architecture and program were conceived as a constant, reiterative process of discovery. Both grew out of a step by step practice that valued the journey equally with the destination. For both, recursive exploratory operations became algorithms for the discovery of significant forms, images, and ideas. These beliefs prompted the architects to fix the building in the specific social nexus of the University's and the city's history and site. This philosophy encouraged them to create a home for the program out of a vocabulary that could be read unambiguously as a narrative, map, and metaphor for historical, aesthetic, and social relationships. And these beliefs established a program that would present art as the repository of ideas, social commentary and social action as well as aesthetic fact. Yet, at the same time that they have been deeply influenced by the postmodern spirit, both the program and the architecture have felt the continuing authority of the modern and have wrestled with the historical tension between modern and postmodern. Neither has withdrawn its faith in the modernist ideology of art and architecture as experimentation and formal discovery. Both relish the random encounter, the new vista, the unexpected. It is at times only with regret that each has given up the comfort of aesthetic idealism.

2. Derived from the program of the University Gallery, the Center saw its role as mirroring in the arts the University's most advanced research centers in engineering, medicine, and theoretical physics. In this context it would present deconstructions of the history and experience of painting as well as canvases of political statement. Its ongoing film series would assiduously investigate the possibilities beyond Hollywood, looking at film's pre-history, alternative culture, and disparate social histories. Feminist concerns and the impact the arts have in empowering women and minorities would be preeminent in the Center's program. The Center would become

the premier showcase in Columbus for the presentation of performance art, new music, and those new art forms whose hallmarks are metacritical analysis, experimentation, mixed-media, and collaboration. The Center would augment the strong collection of early seventies post-minimal, conceptual, and decorative works assembled by Betty Collings, and the work of social and political conscience which I added to the collection, by building a collection out of recent directions in painting, film, video, photography, architecture, media, and installation art; work which is increasingly interdisciplinary and related to such fields as linguistics, economics, history, and anthropology.

During the construction of the building, as an indication of the directions the program would take, the University Gallery produced three Preview events: The acoustic environment, Pink Noise, was a specially commissioned collaboration by the composer Philip Glass and the sculptor Richard Serra. As an extension of the installation the Philip Glass Ensemble gave the Midwest premiere of the five hour work Music in Twelve Parts. This work addressed issues of the nature of the boundaries between the media of sculpture and music. The Gallery also looked at two of the most demanding social issues in Rape and AIDS: The Artists' Response. Rape, *the first show of its kind, elicited sustained commentary, provided a vehicle for workshops, and acted as a catalyst for increased social consciousness.* AIDS: The Artists' Response *brought to Columbus an exhibition of art, over fifty hours of videotapes, a national symposium, and the Names Project Quilt. And as a direct response to the architecture,* 12 1/4 Degrees: Primary Access *was produced on the active building site. This dance and new music work used both New York and Columbus dancers, choreographers, musicians, and the Center's construction workers (as dancers) to explore issues of scale, the site as dance stage and sound surround, and the tension between the unfinished and the expectation of completion. As these activities demonstrated, the Center's programs would be derived from a repetitive investigation of collaboration, social inquiry, and formal experimentation. The result of some projects would be unpredictable. The risk of failure would be high. But such an investigative process—the exhibition program's algorithm for discovery—possessed the potential for reaching into new territories and encountering the new and the genuine.*

3. To the first time viewer, the Center will undoubtedly provoke two distinct responses. As one moves from the relatively serene, almost traditionally landscaped exterior of the building to the interior walkways there is a growing sense of modernism gone wild: of some bizarre cohabitation of the modern and the surreal. The building aggressively reverses recent museum strategies of eclectic exteriors balanced by minimalist interiors—as in Arata Isozaki's Los Angeles MOCA. At Ohio State the lobby, ramps, baroquely patterned glass spine, and galleries appear to be chaotic geometric fragments. Stairs lead to nowhere. Columns are cut off in midair or plunge into the middle of a grand stairway. Here geometric intrusions, like stalactites, hang from above, making a passage seem claustrophobic or impeding the view. And the galleries contain the structural deconstructions of the modernist White Cube. Projecting from the wall and embedded in ceiling and floor are the Cube's component parts, each disconnected from the whole and set out in space as in an exploded drawing of machine parts. Or, perhaps another experience is the building's particular sense of unity, revealed with growing clarity as one moves from outside into the interior walkways, theaters and galleries. One begins to sense relationships between site and landscape, outside and inside. One becomes quickly aware of the repetitive, rhythmic elements of the geometry. Their modulation seems to correspond to a complex meditation on the meaning of presentation and public space.

The conflict at the basis of this project is very real. It is the sustained clash between the high modern desire for isolation and pure form—the building as sculpture—and the postmodern obligation to relevance and context. The achievement of the architecture is its ability to ratify both the postmodern and the modern references: the socio-political meaning of the program and the site, and the tectonic power of architectural form. This achievement is underwritten formally and conceptually by an ingenious, radically revisionist use of the archetypal modernist element, the grid. Rather than the singular modernist grid—with its epistemological connotations of the anti-material and the anti-mimetic, and its political connotations of the regimented—the architects chose to use as the essential seed for the project not a single grid but the overlay of two grids. These two grids derive figuratively from the geometries of the campus and the city. More profoundly they are captured whole from actuality. Their geometries lie within the real world, within a real site. Their existence contains and encompasses an astonishing multiplicity of meanings and connections. Choosing their overlap and intersection as the project's basis provided in one fell swoop both the architectural matrix and the broadest range of historical and socio-political references. This bold stroke confirmed both mathematical model and metaphor. It provided the potential for mapping and representing the complexities of the real and the conceptual. Early in the design proposal the architects allowed the grids to shear, to shadow, and to fracture; they sensitively weighed and orchestrated their reappearance and disappearance. By doing so they arrived at a system of enormous flexibility. What the overlapping grids then produced was not a singular, given relationship, but rather the potential for relationships. This system liberated the architects from the ideology of the White Cube, allowing them to embody the program in a spatial continuum in which each part mirrored and reiterated aspects of the whole. No longer was the room the basis of the exhibition program, no longer were galleries necessarily rooms.

This system provided a variable algorithm for the discovery of new forms and for the architectural embodiment of the program. This system acted as a propagating procedure that constantly generated new formal and spatial relationships. Its fractal-like potential provided a method against which the formulation and meaning of each element could be tested, adjusted, balanced, and refined. The system established a process of discovery and exploration. It allowed for modulation in the formal vocabulary of the building. It made the design development paradigmatic of the most responsive creative acts.

Throughout the architecture there are commanding demonstrations of clarity and humanity; grand moments in which the building most clearly succeeds both as formal statement and as an extraordinary home for the program. On the exterior, these are embodied in elements that emphasize human scale and passage. Initially it was thought that the reconstructed Armory would become the building's signature. Yet, in the completed building its resurrection is overshadowed by the fabricated landscape. Both tower and building play secondary roles to the plinths *and passageways. The entire site is transformed into an enormous earthwork. The building elements become only aspects in the massing of earth forms. They become a series of sculptural elements which repeat on the exterior the programmatic requirements of the interior. To walk through the site is to experience a variety of scale, clarity of vista, and invitation to passage rarely felt in the urban environment. The plinths, the slowly rising grid of the scaffolding, and the floating roof top extrusion are more than just metaphors for the land and the horizon. Their modulated scale and volume, undulating planting, color and physical material, and ability to open and frame new, lucid prospects, become the broad, democratic, Midwestern landscape itself.*

The bright precision of the exterior is transformed inside into a more energetic landscape. Once the lower lobby is entered, the interior spreads out before the viewer as both plain and skyline. The narrow ascending ramp to the galleries provides introduction and a vista of the entire length of the building. From the far end of this ramp the reciprocal view is even more powerful: modulated by the play of light from the clerestory and glass-enclosed spine, the three upper galleries flow into one another, their cascading, geometric forms producing moments of openness and closure. This is a splendid landscape for suspended sculpture, exhibition, and display. Here, the aggressive interventions of the grid create individual districts and environments. These precincts, and the height, volume, and continuous open expanse above the galleries reiterate the building's core meaning: the possibility for insight, and vision. In these galleries, the architecture aggressively articulates the program, providing a flexible series of unique display spaces: sliding walls can be drawn to darken the north gallery into which a projection booth beams slides, film, audio or video; modular, freestanding exhibition walls can further divide and personalize the space. Rather than the minimal, characterless galleries of the high modern, here we are confronted by social, formal, and human elements. Even the wall itself, that most essential and impenetrable of traditional gallery elements, is never presumed. At one place it gives way to vista, at another to ramp, at another it fractures into a column or into multiple planes. The effect of this is to suggest a host of alternatives, a compendium of styles rather than a single endorsed form, an open cinematic, rather than a closed hierarchic system of exhibition presentation, an egalitarian rather than an elite art.

The black box Performance Theater at the northern end of the building is perhaps the building's most exceptional and speculative space. Here the requirement for height and clear span necessitated new permutations of the grid system. The grid necessarily has to wrap the space. In this wrapping it takes on a ingenious variety of manifestations: cat walk, stairway, mezzanine, stretch wire grid, acoustic wall grill. Traditional fixed theater elements give way to modular, mobile gear and seating and equipment that allow for performance flexibility. This is a theater of investigation and experimentation: its meaning is embedded in the inventiveness and responsiveness of the architecture. In the Film Theater at the opposite end of the building the generative aspects of the Performance Space are reinvestigated and re-articulated. Indeed, the entire building is a study in self-similar modulated form. Throughout the building an algorithmic repetition ceaselessly reveals new formal solutions to programmatic requirements.

4. The opening of the Center for the Visual Arts marks the fruition and extension of experiments and investigations within the Gallery program, and by the Center's architects. Yet, its opening presents a critical juncture in the Center's life and a test for its long term potential. Begun as the University Gallery—an idealistic, democratized means of bringing new work and new ideas to the university—the Center's new stature and visibility, its larger audience potential, and its landmark status, may make it difficult to retain the program's integrity. It is paradoxical that the architects' success in transforming the public space of the university with a radical gesture could neutralize that space, precluding its use for other experimental projects. Yet I strongly believe the architecture will prevail. The investigative process set in motion by the program and the architecture will continue to provoke new discoveries. As the competition jury wrote over six years ago, "The scheme provokes speculation and almost relishes the idea of uncertainty." Embedded in the algorithm of the architecture is text, prototype, and program that will proclaim art's humanity, social responsibility, and investigative power.

COUNTER-MONUMENTS IN PRACTICE: THE WEXNER CENTER FOR THE VISUAL ARTS

Anthony Vidler

An age that has deflated its values and lost sight of its purposes will not produce convincing monuments.
Lewis Mumford [1]

In a recent article on the competition for the Ohio State University Center for the Visual Arts, Kurt Forster intimated that the quandary of contemporary architecture may be measured according to architects' responses to institution building, and especially to that of the museum. Forced to choose between "an idolatrous re-creation of the past 'temple of the arts' on the one side; an amusement park of cultural recreation on the other," architects were in neither case able to respond to a condition of flux. Forster concluded in favor of the solution by Eisenman/Trott that, in his words, was "all process rather than product," as against other solutions that attempted a more traditional monumentality.[2]

But if this opposition was evident in the competition designs, and reinforced by the distinctly different discourses of the entering architects, the built realization of a scheme founded on indeterminacy and process raises the question of monumentality once again and in a more paradoxical way. A project established according to premises of the impermanent has become permanent; a form developed out of a criticism of monumentality has been, so to speak, instantly monumentalized.

Such a dilemma poses special problems for the finished building, now unsupported by helpful text, and bound to categories of empirical experience. In the context of Peter Eisenman's designs, this question is rendered even more acute as the theoretical and specifically anti-monumental parti pris has been imposed from the outset. If monuments, classically speaking, might be defined in Siegfried Giedion's words, as "human landmarks which men have created as symbols for their ideals, for their aims, and for their actions," then Eisenman has consistently worked against such a concept.[3] But if, as Hegel insisted, the work of art is defined by the meaning attached to formed material by culture, then what is to prevent the process being reversed, so that a building, not intended to be a monument, once deprived of its author, might be interpreted by society as monumental? How might the critical premises of counter-monumentality survive in the face of the human will to force meaning onto objects whatever the objections of their makers?

Monuments

Thus the great monuments are raised up like dikes, opposing the logic of majesty and authority to every troubled element. Georges Bataille [4]

In this way Bataille attempted to account for the power of monuments, tracing their effect to the very architectonic structure of power in

society, comparing their character to the physiognomies of hieratic officials. For Bataille, it was the presence of architectural composition itself, underlying all the traditional arts, that signalled authority, whether exhibited in physiognomy, costume, music or painting: "the grand compositions of certain painters express the will to constrain the spirit with an official ideal." Monuments, he argued, were "the true masters of the entire earth, grouping in their shadow the servile masses: It is under the form of cathedrals and palaces that the Church or the State address and impose silence on the masses. It is evident, in effect, that monuments inspire social wisdom and often even a veritable fear."[5]

To be condemned to such authority was, indeed, like being condemned to the galleys. The taking of the Bastille in the French Revolution could be explained, in this way, as an expression of "the animosity of the people against the monuments that are its true masters."

Monuments, indeed, took their place quite naturally in the ordered development of society, by virtue of the fact that their origin— the imposition of mathematical order on stone—was accomplished by evolution itself, by the passage from the "simian form to the human form, which latter already presented all the elements of architecture."[6] The anthropomorphic dependence of architecture on the body is here given a new twist by Bataille. Architecture is now seen as an organic part of the biological development, the "morphological process," in which man is forlornly stranded as a mere intermediate stage between monkeys and great buildings. Architectural order, developed out of human order, is of a higher kind; thence the power of monuments.

Such a characterization of monumentality, as the very definition of the role and nature of architecture, succinctly summarized the classical monumental tradition at a moment when such monumentality was itself under attack from technocratic and idealist modernists alike. Bataille himself noted that with the disappearance of the architectonic substructure of the art work—that "kind of dissimulated architectural skeleton"— the way was opened to the expression of psychological processes, profoundly incompatible with social stability. Only the movement away from the elegance of the human figure, architectural in essence and therefore dominated by architecture, and towards a form of "bestial monstrosity" might, Bataille concluded, provide a chance of escaping the architectural penitentiary.

Writing in 1929, Bataille was of course intervening in a continuing debate that had pitted modernists, calling for a "new monumentality" as opposed to the "pseudomonumentality" of eclectic historicism (to use Siegfried Giedion's terms), against nostalgics and traditionalists who mourned the passing of the grand epochs of monumental splendor, and saw little hope in the cultural forms of the declining west. In this debate, Bataille deliberately confused the terms, ascribing to all monumentality the architectural will to power, and finding the only remedy in the complete rejection of architecture, at least as traditionally defined. Tristan Tzara and Salvador Dalì, among others, were to advance this position in articles published in Minotaur, outlining the possibilities of a psychoanalytically theorized architecture of hysteria, of digestion, or of the uncanny, intra-uterine cave. In each case, the tradition of geometry was opposed by a psycho-formal sensibility that once more assimilated architecture to the natural. The monstrous half-natural, half-cultural was posed as a counter to the abstract and the rational.

Sixty years later, Bataille's gently ironic attack on monumentality that called for the dissolution of architectural order and the irruption of the monstrous as the only defense against the virtually Darwinian law of the monuments, takes on a new cast. In the context of a quarter-century of attempts to revive a perceived "lost monumentality," with an attendant proliferation of the pseudomonumental to a degree unimagined even by Giedion, the question of the architectural monument as dissimulated power, has been raised again in a strangely attenuated form. In this context, it has now become evident that a simple argument against, say, historical quotation or stylistic revival, and in favor of a vague "modernity," easily falls into the trap anticipated by Bataille; both post-modern and late-modern evince a nostalgia of form, both seek a lost architecture, both attempt to achieve monumentality and thereby domination. To pose the question in other terms, however, would, as Bataille intimated, involve an absolute rupture with the architectonic tradition and, by implication, the "body" on which that tradition was based and that it dominated.

Counter-Monuments
Certain architects have advanced possible forms of this counter-monumental argument. Some, like Coop Himmelblau, have preferred a textual mode, illustrating the idea of the non-monumental, the grotesque, the uncanny, in arresting graphic images; others, like Hejduk, have explored the surrealist legacy, attempting to configure a "monstrous" double for architecture that would privilege the victim over the victor. Others, like Libeskind, have turned to different formal models—impossible machines, decomposed bodies—as the emblems of an abyss no architecture can finally heal. Some, like Gehry, have embraced a bricolage populism that attempts to underplay the monumental in favor of the apparently accidental.

In this field of possibilities, the approach of Peter Eisenman (and in this context Eisenman/Trott) has been especially tantalizing. Founded on a discourse of rupture with the classical-humanist past, a post-apocalyptic vision of a world inhabited by absence and uncertainty, his projects have progressively explored the dimensions of the counter-architectural. Rejecting the authority drawn by classicism from fixed and stable origins—origins in need, in use, in anthropomorphism, in aesthetic formulae—Eisenman's work has moved from an initial reliance on the vocabulary of modernism in the House series, to a more radical assumption of architecture's demise, for example the excavations and almost geological mappings of later projects like that for the Romeo and Juliet castles, or the Progressive Corporation project in Cleveland, Ohio.

Exemplified in projects and presented in complicated self-analytical graphics and models, these designs have remained hypotheses in the fabrication of a counter-monumental myth—untested by being built, comfortably surrounded by a textual discourse that, by metonymy, imply their radicality and assimilates them to the cause.

In the case of The Ohio State University Wexner Center for the Visual Arts, this fragile compact between text and project, between criticism and design, has been definitively broken. The building rises from the ground, ready for inhabitation, to assume its place among a series of monumental constructions around the formal periphery of the campus center, standing for and set in the institutional structure of the university. Sited between two already existing monuments, themselves clothed in the stripped classical style of Giedion's "pseudomonumentality," how could such a building, if only as a result of its shear physical bulk and material presence, not participate in the monumentality that surrounds it and that, institutionally, if not formally, defines the reason for its existence?

At first glance, indeed, the building seems to aspire to and achieve a monumentality of impeccable proportions. With its brick faced castellated frontispiece, its arched recesses mimicking the original armory and its majestically rhythmic three-dimensional grids forming closed and open arcades, and its sensitive interstitial connections to the existing auditoria, the Center takes on the appearance of a carefully contextualized institutional complex. Whether viewed from the Oval, or from the entrances to the campus, the building sits, elegant and pristine, its brilliant white matrices and deep red brick surfaces scaled perfectly to its environs. Its presence is undeniable.

Yet this image of certain stability, of monumental power, is immediately undermined in a number of increasingly unsettling ways. First, the "entrance" through the re-constructed armory tower is revealed on closer inspection not to be an entrance at all; its huge arch is blocked and sunken, as if some ancient fortification had been closed off as unsafe. Further, the brick mass of this ostensibly historical "restoration" is peeled back in layers, as if sliced by a surgical scalpel, to reveal a sequence of shifting surfaces that effectively break any illusion of security. The once stable historical fragment emerges as an elaborate commentary on temporal destabilization. The ruinating work of time is replicated in simulacrum as a complex play between the restored and the de-restored.

Secondly, the grids that form the body of the building itself, calibrated on three measures—twelve, twenty-four and forty-eight feet—seem to operate independently of and entirely distinctly from either structure or spatial enclosure. They quite evidently work against any resolution, even one of a dialectic between, say, support and enclosure as in the free plan, explicitly refusing any comfortable reconciliation of the two. Indeed, at times, as in the open "arcade" (that itself performs no sheltering function) that runs between the existing auditorium and the new structure, or in the intersection of the largest grid with the narrow internal stairs, the grids clash with any intimation of occupation and use, and sometimes with each other, with deliberate abruptness.

The "monument" here gradually dissolves into a series of discreet fragments—of replicated history, of grids and structures—that uncomfortably touch, intersect or break into each other with no overall unity save that of metonymic resonance.

Such fragmentation has recently been compared to the structural expressionism and a-classical composition of Russian constructivism, based on superficial resemblances of clashing axes and grids. But there is little affinity between the Russian examples, deliberately distorting and scrambling the codes of classicism while exalting the potentials of steel and reinforced concrete structure, and the abstract and distanced grids of the Wexner Center. In the first place, the Eisenman/Trott grids do not in fact stand for structure. They are simply built grids that are their own structure but that do not coincide at every point with the real structure of the building, nor do they symbolize any structural potential of architecture. They are not, in this sense, images of the "origins" of architecture conceived of as essential structure, nor are they signs of the absence of this origin. Rather, they stand for another, less stable origin, one that lies in the geometrization of territory.

Each grid is itself shifted according to a different axial direction taken from already existing mappings on the site or its context. Clues are drawn from at least two mapped directions latent in the site: that of the town of Columbus, and that of the campus itself. A further reference to mapping lies in the "fault" line cutting through the building, an echo of the Greenville trace cutting through Ohio itself. Each built grid is then, so to speak, envisaged in three-dimensional space and built up from the ground as a realization of the virtual. The conflicts between grids then, are not compositionally *generated*; rather they are latent in their hypothetical occupation of the same site, and are explicitly brought to light only by the constructed attempt to occupy the same site with three different contents.

Grids
In this sense, the nature of the grids deployed in the Wexner Center departs radically from the traditional use of grids in architecture. Grids, in the classical tradition, have generally been utilized for two complementary purposes: for the composition, layout and arrangement of elements of architecture in space—the instrumental grid—such as that employed in drafting or in surveying, and for the manifestation of structure in modeled or real space, as in a column grid. Modernism altered this dualism very little: the instrumental grid became more pervasive with the introduction of graph paper and the mass production of architectural elements, and the structural grid became revealed as an integral part of the abstract "essence" of architecture, but the double representational status of the grid remained. Generally, the two kinds of grids were virtually synonymous in practice, especially in the work of Mies van der Rohe where instrumental and structural grids coincided as the basis for an abstract language of structure. Even in more overtly metaphysical projects, such as those of de Stijl architects, the grid was seen, by Rosalind Krauss, in her seminal essay "Grids," first published in October in 1979, as mediating between a necessary "coordinate system for mapping the real," and a "staircase to the Universal."[7] Whether physically or metaphysically instrumental, modernist grids were utilized precisely because of this dualism, and, even more importantly, for the implied correspondance between the grid and the essentially architectonic.

In Eisenman's work, however, the grid seems to signal none of these connotations. Tied neither to instrumental reason, nor to a transcendental other world, the Wexner grid stands as the merciless demonstration, as it were, of conflict in the mapping of the real, while it definitively rejects any essentialist message with regard to the structural or spatial nature of architecture. On the one hand manifested in the form of a set of apparently arbitrarily located fragments precipitated out of a potentially unlimited field, and on the other defining the physical limits of the structure, the grid seems to hover between the infinite and the bounded, ambiguous and refusing all narratives of a single point of origin.

Rosalind Krauss has remarked on this dualistic nature of the grid, at once centrifugal and centripetal in implication. The grid, she argues, makes the work of art a fragment by virtue of its infinite extendibility from the work of art outward; the art-work thus becomes "a tiny piece arbitrarily cropped from an infinitely larger fabric." At the same time, as a definer of the outer limits of the aesthetic object, the grid appears as "an introjection of the boundaries of the world into the interior of the work" here the grid appears as "a mapping of the space inside the frame onto itself... a mode of repetition."[8] In the three-dimensional realm of the architectural grid, these two conditions have generally oscillated: a traditional humanism, such as that evinced by Palladio, has taken the grid metaphysically as a fragment of infinity and physically as a container and centralizing property; modernism broke this defined oscillation to provoke ambiguity so that, for example, in the case of a composition by Theo van Doesburg, the conceptual grid is infinite, and the realized grid is both centripetal and centrifugal, the one pointing to the potential of the other.

In the Eisenman/Trott scheme this dualistic condition of the modernist grid still seems operative—the fragmentary grids reach out to infinity and their edges limit the object's boundaries—but any clear dialectical reading, such as that enabled by the paintings of Mondrian, has been thwarted in two ways. First, the conceptual field—that of the infinite grid—has been a priori disrupted by the intrusion of more than one grid. The calm and pristine state of the "universal" has been transformed into an abyssal conflict among a potentially infinite number of grids struggling for primacy. The regular and geometrical prison of Bataille's "architecture" has been reformulated as a battle field of infinite difference that refuses repetition or similarity from the outset. The conceptual field is thus composed of so many possible human errors of mapping, and is no longer a "universal" in the transcendental sense offered by classicism or modernism.

Secondly, nothing in the conflicted play of these fragments of the non-universal indicates that the boundaries of the object logically and centripetally work their way towards a meaningful center. There is indeed, no such center, each axis, once started on the interior, dissolves into or is broken by another. Reinforcing this impression, the "rooms" or "spaces" within the center repeat the confusion and conflict of fragments and grids while at every moment resisting a centralizing reading. If, as Rosalind Krauss asserts, "behind every twentieth-century grid there lies—like a trauma that must be repressed—a symbolist window parading in the guise of a treatise on optics,"[9] behind the Eisenman/Trott grids lie the ruins of modernist grids, ruins that are by no means suppressed like a trauma, but that are brought into the light of their own contradictions.

Schizographies

Because of its bivalent structure (and history) the grid is fully, even cheerfully, schizophrenic.
Rosalind Krauss[10]

The simple schizophrenic character of the grid noted by Krauss is in Eisenman's work pulled from a state of traumatic repression into expression. Jacques Lacan, writing in 1931, spoke of such expressions, valuable for psychoanalytical practice, "not only as symptoms of profound troubles in thought, but also as revelations of their evolving stage and of their interior mechanism."[11] The manifestation of these "more or less incoherent forms of language" was named "schizophasia"; their written counterparts, Lacan termed "schizography." Akin to that "automatic writing" studied with so much care by nineteenth century mystics, schizography, as defined by Lacan, would be the study of written or spoken disturbances in normal writing or speech. Lacan analyzes cases of elision, denegation, neologism, displacement and the like in order to demonstrate that, rather than ascribing such disorders to the "inspirational" or mystical category, one should see in them the demonstration on a linguistic level of the disorder itself.

Reading Eisenman's schizophrenic grids in this light, we might be tempted to see the conflation of conflicting fragments, evidence of a deliberate evocation of a schizographic condition (inherent in the world more than in the author) that works with the "methods" of the paranoiac in order to reveal a "real" disturbingly disturbed. Here we might follow Lacan himself, as he compared the schizographies of his patients—in which "depending on the intellectual and cultural level of the patient, happy conjunctions of images could be produced episodically giving a highly expressive result"—to those more self-conscious experiments in automatism conducted by the "surrealists," and that exploited play as a state of oscillation between intention and automatism.[12] But more revealing still was Lacan's conclusion that the most common characteristic of schizographic disturbance was a heterogeneous conjuncture of the "waste products (les scories) of consciousness, words, syllable, obsessive sonorities, catch-phrases, assonances, different automatisms: everything that a thought in a state of activity, that is, which identifies the real, repulses and annuls by a judgement of value."

Placed on the level of the intentional blurring of the planned and the automatic, we might now be able to read Eisenman's insistence on the automatic nature of his grid generation—an automatic transcription of previous geometrical mappings—together with his evident pleasure in manipulating the conflicts in this "real," as a conscious schizography. Further, in his use of simulated fragments of history, at once marking previous sites of architectural and institutional occupation and fabricating shifted and cut apart versions of this history, Eisenman seems to be utilizing the scoria—literally the "slag"—of architectural tradition in order to fabricate a counter, necessarily schizophrenic, architecture.

Here we are returned to Bataille's initial desire to counter architecture with the monstrous, form with the formless. By rupturing architecture's link with anthropomorphic imitation, Eisenman has broken with its tradition of form, has produced something that, in existing cultural terms, has no recognizable form, and moreover has worked insistently to counter any idea of "form" wherever it might arise.

In his note on the word "formless,"[13] Bataille advanced the philosophical explanation for his position on architecture: "formless" was a word, he noted, that was normally employed to denote a will to form, a loss of status in a universe where everything ought to have form:
In effect, in order for academic men to be content, the universe ought to have form. Philosophy in its entirety has no other aim: it is concerned with giving a frock-coat to what is, in itself, the frock-coat of mathematics.[14]

"Formless" would be in this context something base, like a spider or an earthworm. Substituting the words architecture and geometry for philosophy and mathematics, we might infer that in Bataille's terms, an architecture that, like a formless universe, resembled nothing on earth, "was something like a spider or a pool of spittle."[15] Perhaps it is in this sense that we might identify the "grotesque" and the "monstrous" in Eisenman's oeuvre. No longer content to dress up a frock-coat in a frock-coat, he prefers instead to reveal the inherently formless in all attempts at fixed and closed form, the schizographic nature of an architecture that refuses its monumental duties by writing out its pathological condition. Where in classical terms a monster might be fabricated out of the untoward mingling of genres, in this quasi-automatic mode, the monstrous is no longer to be repressed by a pre-conceived code, but rather explored as the necessary precondition of post-apocalyptic society. Architecture might then become, once more, in Bataille's fomulation "the expression of the very being of society," and the architect might work like Bataille's modernist painters who opened the way "towards bestial monstrosity; as if there was no other chance of escaping from the architectural chain-gang."[16]

1. Lewis Mumford, "Monumentalism, Symbolism and Style," Architectural Review *(April, 1949)*, *179*, quoted in Siegfried Giedion, Architecture, You, Me, *Cambridge, Mass.: Harvard University Press, 1958, 23.*

2. Kurt W. Forster, "Traces and Treason of a Tradition. A Critical Commentary on Graves' and Eisenman/Robertson's Projects for the Ohio State University Center for the Visual Arts, A Center for the Visual Arts, The Ohio State University Competition, *New York: Rizzoli International Publications, 1984, 135.*

3. Siegfried Giedion, J.L. Sert, F. Leger, "Nine Points on Monumentality," *(1943), in Giedion,* Architecture, You, Me, *Cambridge, Mass.: Harvard University Press, 1958, 48.*

4. Georges Bataille, "Architecture," Oeurves completes, *I, Paris: Gallimard, 1970, 171, first published in* Documents, *number 2, May, 1929, 117.*

5. Ibid.

6. Ibid.

7. Rosalind E. Krauss, "Grids," The Originality of the Avant-Garde and Other Modernist Myths, *Cambridge, Mass.: MIT Press, 1985, 10.*

8. Ibid., 18-19.

9. Ibid., 17.

10. Ibid., 18.

11. Jacques Lacan, "Ecrits inspires: Schizographic," De la psychose paranoique dans ses rapports avec la personnalite, *Paris, 1975, 365-382.*

12. Ibid., 379.

13. Bataille, Documents.

14. Ibid., 217.

15. Ibid.

16. Ibid., 172.

UNEXPECTED COINCIDENCES
Rafael Moneo

Peter Eisenman's work before 1978 did not pay much attention to issues of site or program. This work—mainly second residences for sophisticated clients—while looking for a clear expression of an abstract architecture, conceptually ignored the circumstances of landscape and site, and with a rather intellectual condescension, largely reduced the needs of daily life. As a result, these early works became both physical representations of abstract structures aimed at enhancing the formal components of theoretical statements, and elaborate drawings attempting to explain the final stages of a project. It is not until House El even Odd that the intention of relating construction and ground first appears as a premonition of what would become a primary element of his recent architecture, the larger scale projects of the 1980s, which relate building to the site or, to be more precise, to the past of the site, and its potential for excavation.

This concern with site and, more recently, program, should be taken as the basis for understanding the recent work. In fact, it is difficult to understand the Ohio State Center for the Visual Arts without talking about the site; just as it is difficult to engage his Romeo and Juliet project in Montecchio without speaking about the literary plot that determined its program. Eisenman's former reluctance to admit that such circumstances affect architecture has, at least implicitly, changed. His work now starts to take shape either from considerations that have contextual issues at their base or from interpretations of the program that allow him to incorporate current literary ideas into architecture. One wonders if this change in attitude was simply his answer to the post-modernist pressure of the late seventies and to the recent interest in incorporating literary criticism into architecture. But one might also understand this new interest in site and program to be the consequence of approaching broader and more complex projects. As a result Peter Eisenman seems to have discovered that architecture needs to include outside parameters in order to be produced, and that only in the frame of its external circumstance does it acquire meaning.

Two projects are, in my view, key to understanding the Ohio State visual arts center: the Cannaregio project for Venice of 1978 and the building at Checkpoint Charlie in Berlin of 1983. When Eisenman approached the Cannaregio project, he undoubtably felt the weight of a city such as Venice. In spite of his previous attempts to produce architecture without circumstantial ties, here he could not escape the dense context of the particular site; the haunting presence of Le Corbusier's Hospital seems to have hovered in his mind. The project starts by considering the encounter between the Corbusian grid and the city. Here Eisenman discovers the value of a specific site. The new space generated by the rotation and extension of the Corbusian grid became an appropriate context to locate House 11a in a series of different scales. It is possible to explain this first exploration of a context from the fact that House 11a used the horizontality of the ground as a virtual plane to define the oppositions which determine its structure. For whatever reason, Cannaregio became the first in a succession of projects in which Peter Eisenman includes a consideration of the ground, usually as a metaphor alluding to time past.

His Venetian experience would prove extremely useful to the Berlin project. On the site, adjacent to Checkpoint Charlie, only three buildings were left standing on a typical block. Working with these remnants of a city and the nearby Berlin Wall, the architect attempted to re-invent a context through a new interpretation. In so doing, Eisenman superimposed the Mercator grid—the most generic of the Earth's applied divisions—on the Berlin urban grid. The encounter of these grids gave the architect a foundation to propose structures and spaces later outlined in the program requirements. Again Eisenman excavated the ground to discover other grids—

this time of the 18th and 19th centuries—and transformed them along with the first two through changes in scale. The project contains both the generic guidelines for planning the ground surface alongside the assumption of the specific realities of the Berlin Wall and the existing buildings. The abstract grid of the earlier projects is introduced here, giving the Berlin project a continuity with the early work without abandoning the specificity of the site.

The Ohio State arts center building competition provided Eisenman with the opportunity to extend his contextual investigations with specific European sites into the American realm. The Mercator grid's presence in the Berlin project can be seen as a fortuitous premonition of the utility of the grid for examining the American urban landscape. It is not necessary to describe the importance that the grid has had in the development of the American landscape. The entire country, and its cities, is tied to this man-made virtual and often non-virtual network. The Jeffersonian grid was the first instrument used to map the then northwest territory (now Ohio) to symbolize the dominance of the frontier. Columbus, Ohio, did not escape this imposition, and its plan reflects the anomalies resulting from the encounters between different systems of grids. The axis of the Oval orients the buildings of the campus, which is 12 1/4 degrees different from the city's grid, creating a shift that allows a distinction between the campus and the surrounding neighborhoods. The axis of the Oval is visually emphasized by the impressive presence of the Library Tower. Mershon Auditorium and Weigel Hall are two existing buildings on the site which are incorporated into the new construction.

Context to Eisenman does not mean conciliation. For him, context means the physical frame that supports the first step into his process of architectural production, and this emphasis on context forces us to reject the idea that his architecture is indifferent to site. He discovered, in Cannaregio and Berlin, a different kind of context, one implicit in the site and its history. As a result, his most recent architecture comes out of the analysis of something that can still be called context. While he is not concerned with the visual issues of traditional contextualism—which are for many the most understandable aspects of context—he bases his architecture on the implicit premises of the site.

At Ohio State Eisenman/Trott's concern for this expanded idea of context has produced some of the most positive aspects of this work. The key issue involves disconnecting the Oval from High Street or, to be more precise, avoiding a direct relationship between the Oval and the street. The visual extension of the diagonal of 15th Avenue into the campus energizes the Oval as well as the block contained by High Street, 17th Avenue, and College Road. The axis of the campus (the axis of the Oval) generates one grid of the new arts center. The two existing buildings, Mershon Auditorium and Weigel Hall, are absorbed in this grid. Based on this grid, Eisenman/Trott's construction refers to and replicates the typical American city. The entire construction becomes a fragment of a city and, as a consequence, it loses the unitary and synthetic image that buildings once had. Here, structures and grids are what our eyes see rather than the references to figural aspects which used to characterize buildings. This most probably is purposefully sought. Eisenman/Trott's architecture emerges as an architectural phenomenon without assuming the condition of a building.

The construction succeeds in dealing with the campus. Avoiding emphasis on the existing classical central axis, the actual character of the space is preserved and the library is allowed to be the major protagonist on the Oval. The strategy of creating a unity within the new construction and the two existing buildings turns out to be quite successful in two ways — one, by preserving both the openness of the Oval, and its integrity, and two, by integrating Mershon Auditorium and Weigel Hall, the isolation of the buildings on the Oval is strengthened. The ambiguous relationship of Mershon and Weigel to the Oval (in fact Mershon Auditorium's alignments relate to North High Street and Weigel's to College Road) is neutralized as soon as the new construction denies that the main issue of its architecture is the way in which it faces the Oval.

The relationship to the Oval is then entrusted to one of the most debatable elements of the scheme, the tower of the Old Armory. This tower ultimately refers the entire construction to the Oval, but in a skewed, oblique position that makes the role of the remainder of the complex secondary to it. But the marginal position that the complex has in relationship to the Oval speaks about a longing for independence that is very necessary, given the premises of the program. The Center belongs at once to the campus and to the city. It wants to provide activities accessible to the students as well as to the entire community and these programmatic premises are properly represented through the marginality of the Oval created by the displacement of the Armory tower.

No matter how useful it is in giving the Center its correct position, the Armory tower raises some of the work's most pregnant questions for those interested in theoretical issues. Why is such an awkward and problematic element present in the scheme of an architect who has always made claims for the abstract condition of the discipline? Obviously the tower introduces the figurative, and even the dimensional terms of reference that architecture inevitably needs, and this helps to establish the dialectic that is the basis of Eisenman's architecture. Without the tower, the grid—the "substance" of his building—would be less visible. The project needed a reminder of a previously well-defined context both to establish the logic of the intervention, and to render it visible. An analysis of the two disparate grids of city and campus provided the key for overlapping of the project grids, and the use of the historical elements provided the figurative elements needed to clarify the presence of the new figures. Loyal to his rejection of a figurative architectural world, Eisenman invites the presence of the literal past. Had Mershon and Weigel been consistent pieces of architecture, he would not have needed the problematic presence of the tower. In other words, I believe both Eisenman and Trott did not find the actual context strong enough to support the projected construction, and so they excavated the past. Should this excavation then be considered a concession? Should we advance the idea that traditional figurative elements are necessary and that if, for some reason, they are suppressed, will they inevitably emerge in one way or another? It is my belief that, in spite of the fact that for some the tower is the most anecdotal episode of the entire project, it becomes crucial for a comprehensive understanding of the Center's architecture.

When Eisenman/Trott initially presented their competition project, the tower was intact, yet already displaced from where it originally stood, but at that point it was unaffected by the grid. Yet by the time of construction, the tower had been broken by the grid; in other words, the grid prevailed. The tower emerges from below grade level as a metaphorical excavation of the past. Alone and broken, the tower loses its literal quality, avoiding any confusion with a simulation of the armory. The tower becomes the architects' invention, a product of his fiction, of a more equivocal and uncertain reality. Thus the tower stands as one of the most significant theoretical points of the project, not only for strategical reasons in the interpretations of the site, but because it marks the actual entrance to the center, as well as the starting point of the gallery. The location of the tower, and its treatment, are perhaps the most crucial decisions in the entire project.

The Ohio State visual arts center is, in my view, an architecture that proceeds from an accurate examination of its context. For Eisenman/Trott, the site has become so important that context must be "invented" if it is inadequate. That means that this architecture is engendered by an analysis and the interpretation of the site or exterior circumstances, and defers to circumstances. But exaggerating the presence of the external context exacts a price. The interior space, both as category and value, becomes secondary. To be more exact, the interior space becomes a surrogate, an outcome, a simple resultant of external circumstances. This is not true throughout the entire construction, and there are episodes, such as the impressively black experimental theatre, that reach a complete degree of autonomy and thereby escape this condition. I would add that there are some breathtaking moments in the galleries and some beautiful aspects of the entrance. Also of beauty are the transitions between the interior and the exterior, and the interstitial condition of the construction, where the manipulation of the graded platforms, a product of the collaboration with Laurie Olin, ties the Center strongly to the ground and avoids an isolated reading of the sharp and well-defined volumes.

Eisenman/Trott's Ohio State University Wexner Center for the Visual Arts raises once more the issue of the relationship between inside and outside in architecture. Should this distinction be a determinant in producing, and consequently in judging, architecture? Attempts have been made to eliminate this distinction. Late Corbusian architecture would be, in my view, a clear example of this attempt. The categories of interior and exterior are absorbed in his architecture by the sheer physicality of the building fabric, in which the screen provided by the glass plays the anecdotal role of establishing a barrier between two different climatic conditions. Therefore the spaces as well as the materials are treated in a continuous way without reflecting specific spatial differences. This implies that human activities can be the same, in indoor and outdoor conditions. A common, unique idea of architecture prevails as the single and exclusive frame for living. I do not think that this is the case in the Center for the Visual

Arts. In my opinion, as has been said above, the building is the result of a very intelligent analysis and interpretation of urban site, which then almost automatically generates the interior condition as a by-product. The result is a sense of continuous adjustments to given spaces which creates a certain tension, which will only be increased when specific functions or uses begin to emerge. The interior spaces work properly when we cannot identify their known elements or anticipate their uses, when they keep their abstract condition without interfering with specific use.

Curiously, the exterior—unlike the interior—supports the abstract elements of the new construction without any reluctance. Can this be explained simply because of the emphasis put on the outside? Two different answers can be given to this question. One is to say that buildings are indifferent to functions and uses, therefore we are able to adapt any activity to them at some price but without grave harm. We know that this is true to a certain extent. The other is to think that Eisenman deliberately renounced a strategy for the interior that he has used in many of his previous works. Indeed, most of his earlier houses are based on strategies that consider the interior space to be the exclusive battlefield of architectural process. Without anticipating an answer, the most fulfilled examples of architecture that I know have always solved this essential dichotomy between inside and outside without giving an absolute preference to one or the other.

However, one could also argue that in the Wexner Center, the idea of specific interior spaces has led to a more generalized spatial order where a careful treatment of the material merges with a highly intellectualized design. Glass becomes a clear protagonist and what had been reduced to graphic elements in Eisenman's earlier work is transformed into actual and perceptible reality by the tangible presence of this material. The grid matrix is extended to the glass enclosing surfaces, producing an infinite set of changing transparencies multiplied by suncast shadows. The grid also is the texture that supports Eisenman's design strategy called "scaling." Never before has his work explored such a strategy so extensively and, indeed, scaling works in this project properly and efficiently. But in my view, the 48 foot grid is less necessary than the 12 and 24 foot grids, and should only be understood as an attempt to show the generality of the process. The visitor becomes materially enveloped by the atmosphere generated by an appropriate use of both materials and design strategies, a property that gives the Center a touch of two of architecture's classical attributes, consistency and coherence.

Eisenman/Trott's Wexner Center for the Visual Arts tests the ability of the theoretical methods to deal with large-scale construction. This analytical attitude allows problems to be approached with a high degree of generality. The insistence on the grid and the architectural strategies which evolve from it have given them the means to create a continuum which can also embody pieces of a disjointed reality. The idea of a single building has vanished, and instead there appears a complex reality closer to the perception of the idea that we have of our cities today rather than towards traditional buildings. The instability of today's cities seems to be reflected in the Center, and that leads me to say that Eisenman's work, without explicitly pretending to do so, replicates the reality of today's cities. Perhaps paradoxically, some of those procedures that Peter Eisenman might like to call deconstructivist are in fact not so far from the formal mechanisms used by cities in a rather unconscious but rational way as they themselves evolve. In other words, it could be said that some devices that Peter Eisenman has explored through the last year were implicit in the strategies assumed by cities in their unconscious development through time. Unexpectedly, Peter Eisenman's research seems to coincide with a description of the actual city. That would explain why, in the end, the Wexner Center at Ohio State has been able to engage itself in such a beautiful and successful dialogue with its surroundings and presages closer contact in the future between Eisenman's projects and the built world.

**SKETCHES
MODELS
PRESENTATION DRAWINGS
WORKING DRAWINGS**

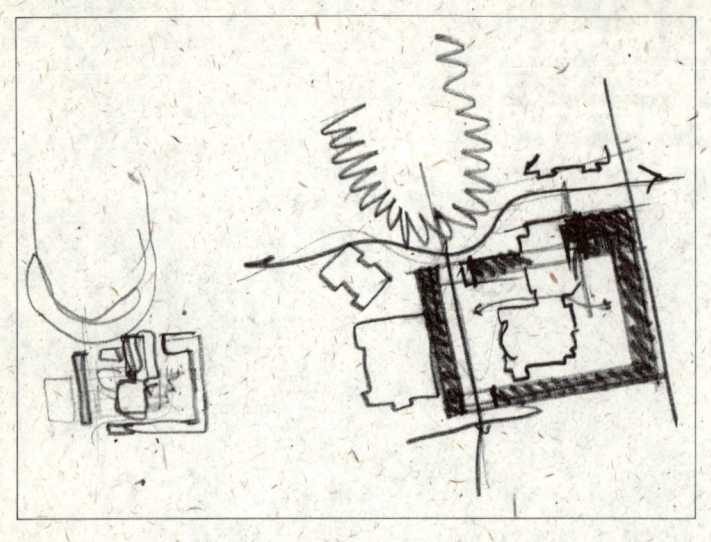

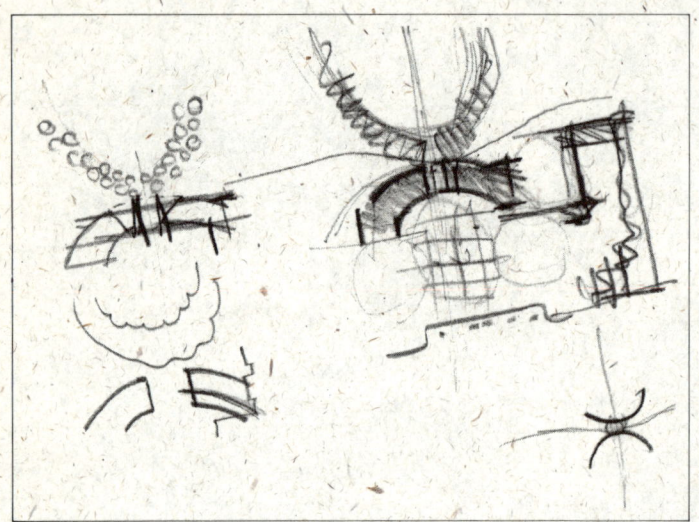
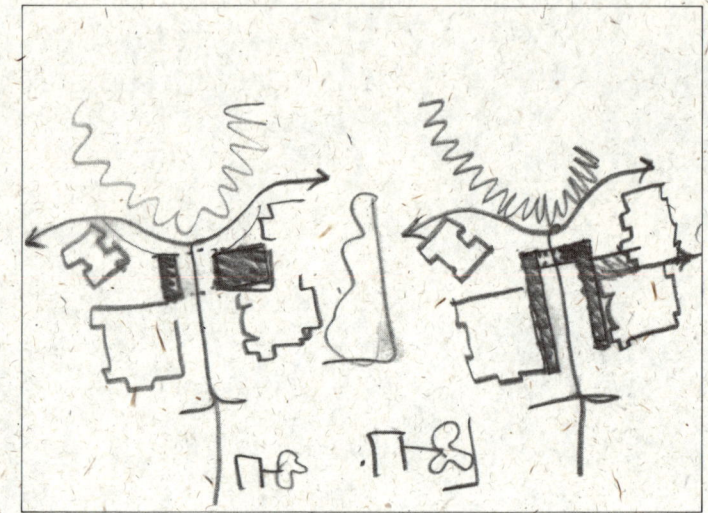

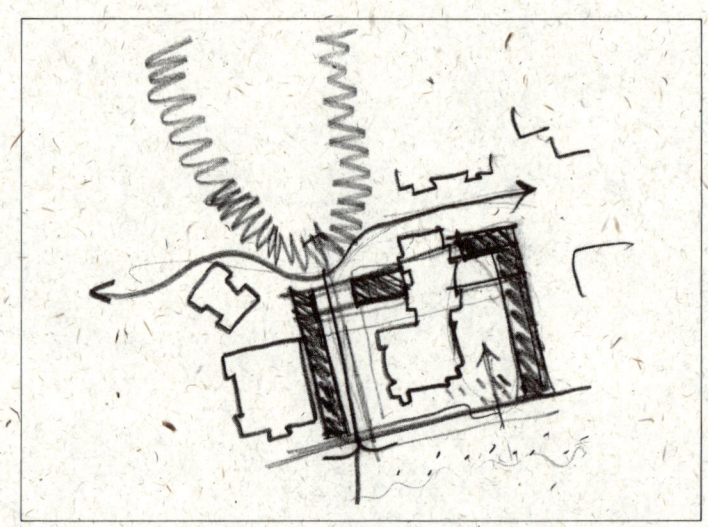

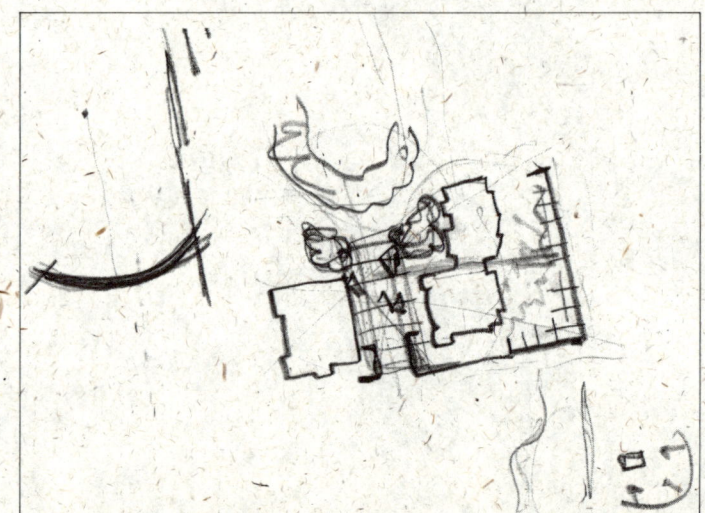

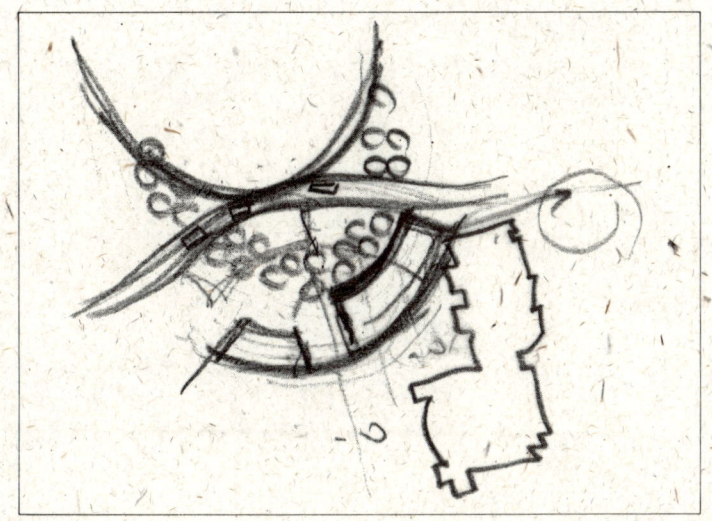
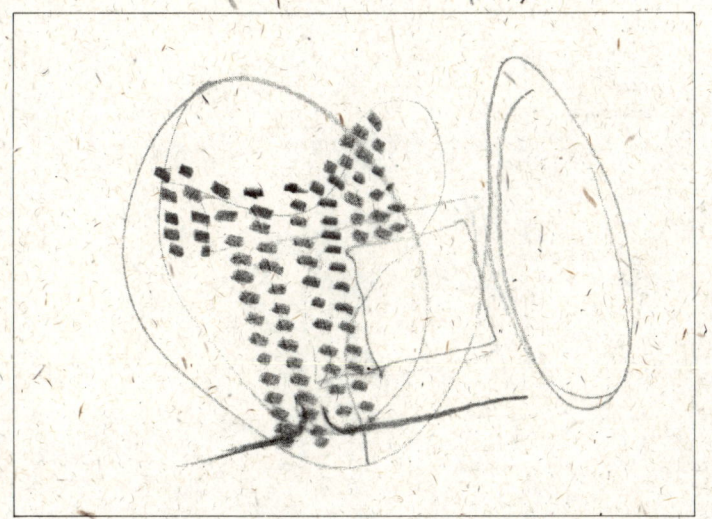

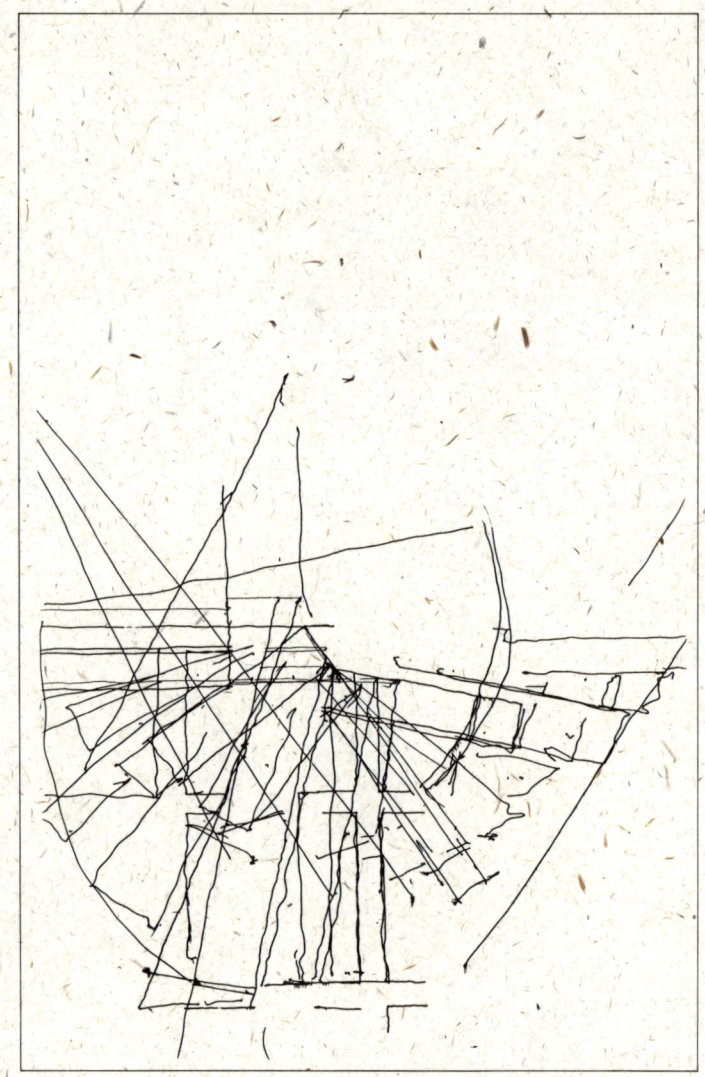

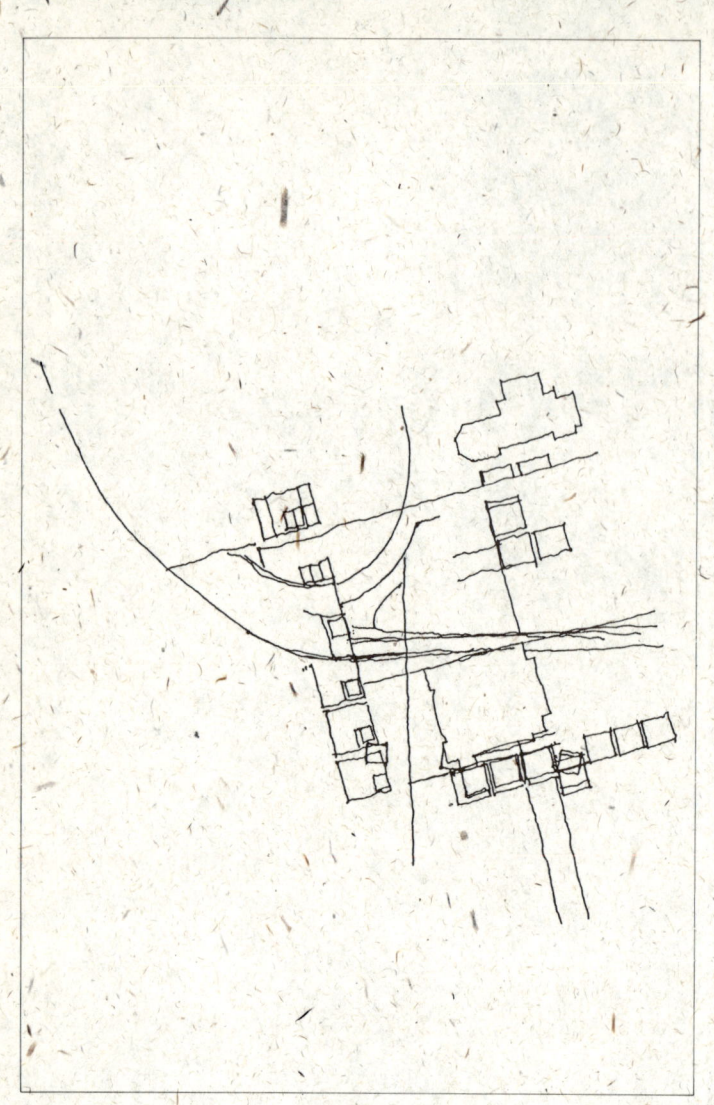
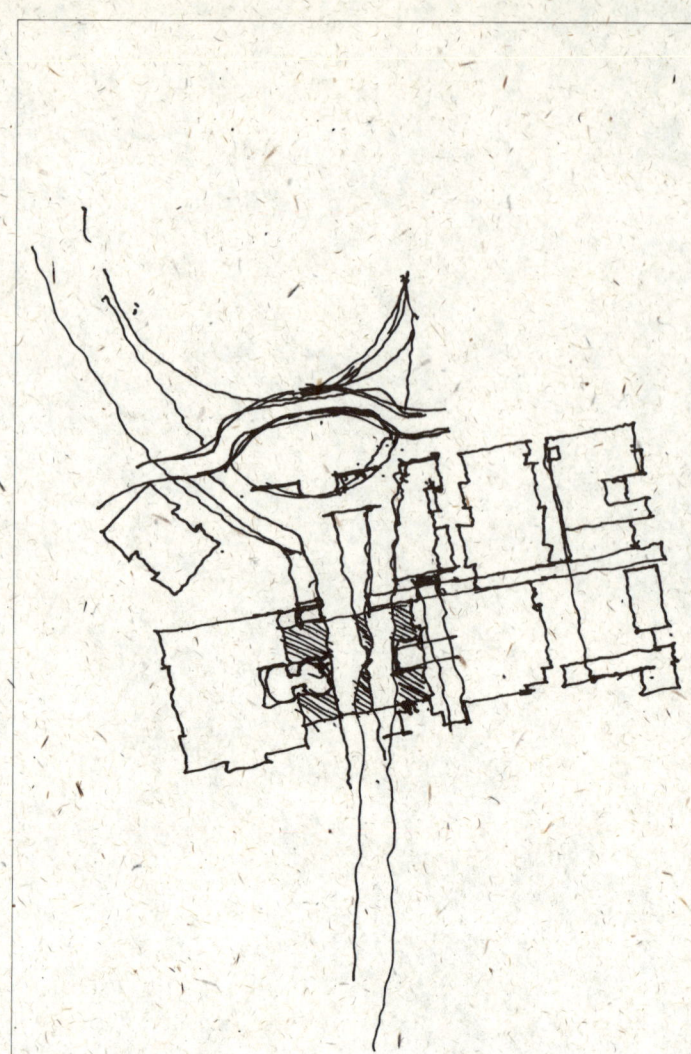

VAC AS — PLANAR LAMENA
OBJECT   MASSIVE REC
CONTAINER
GROUND

26 FEB 83

22 MAR 83
OSU

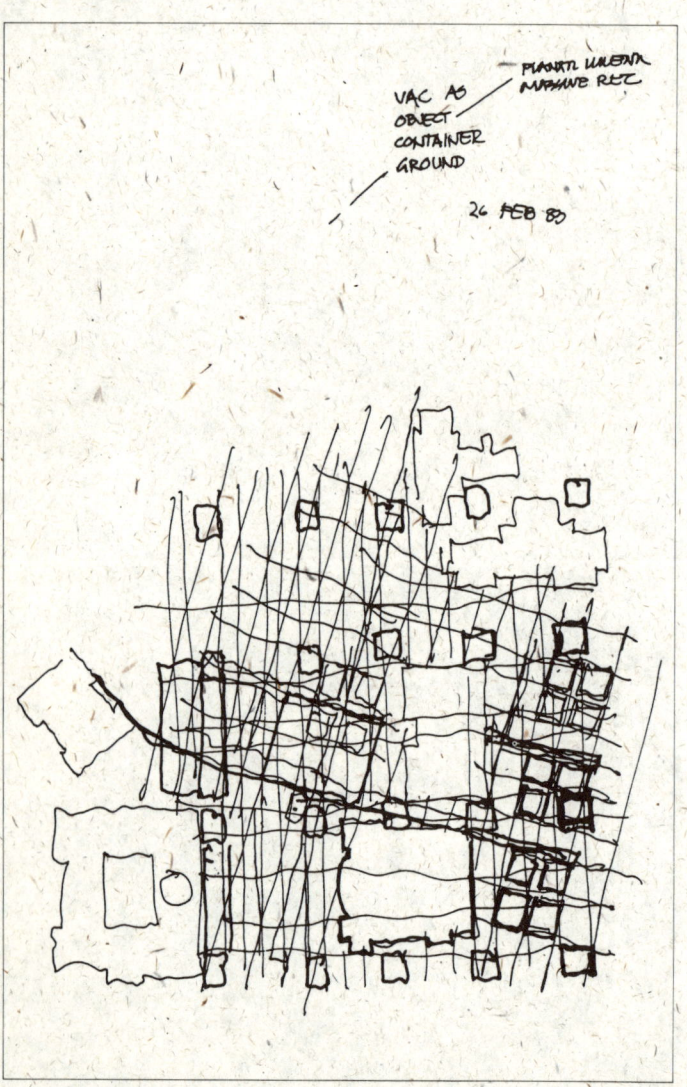
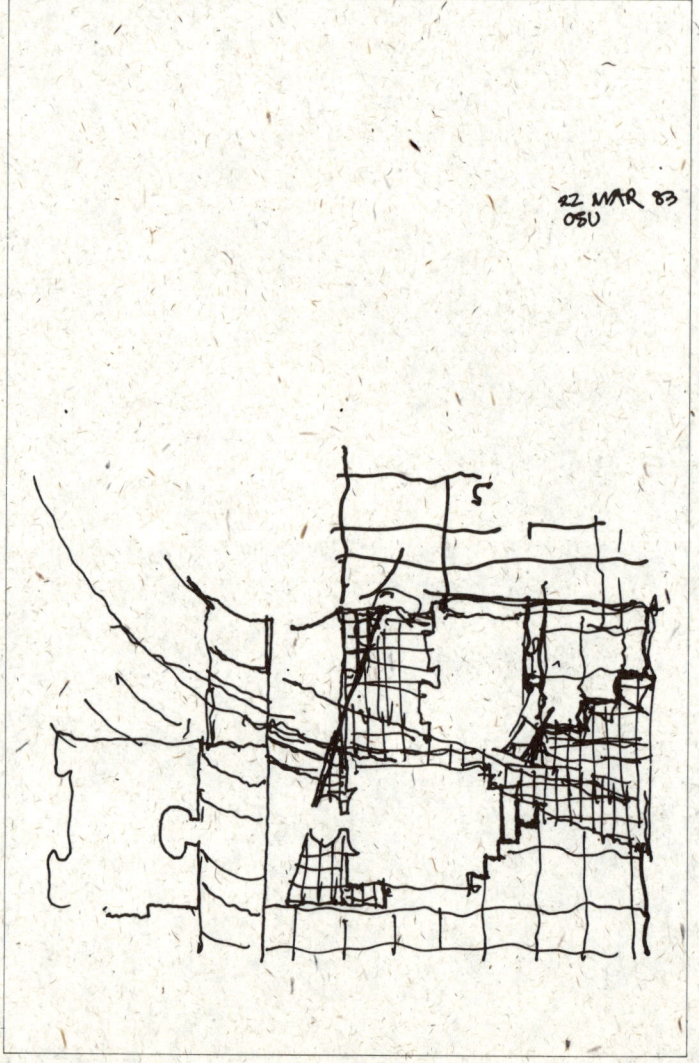

16 FEB 83
OBVAC

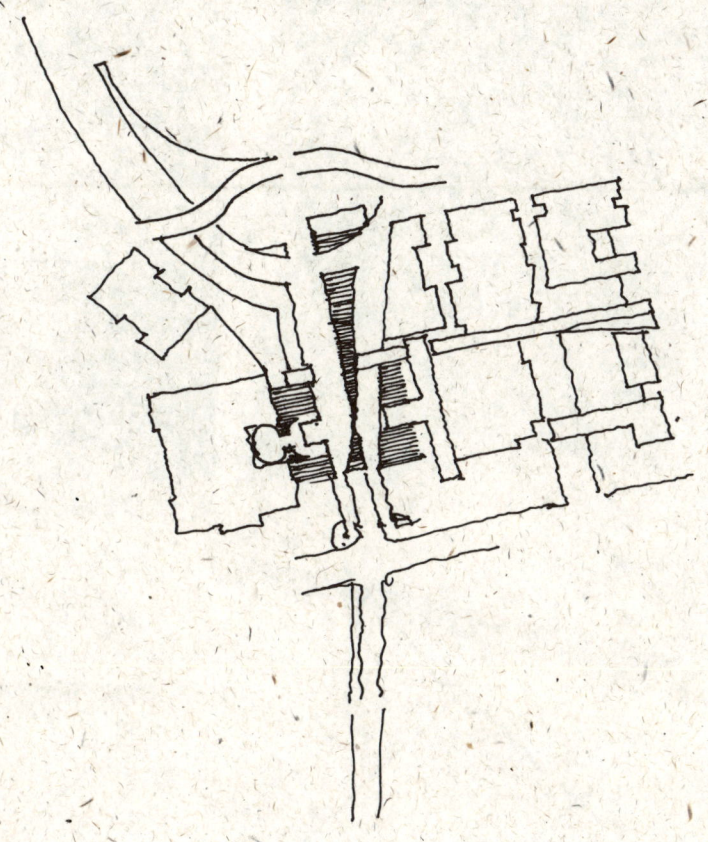

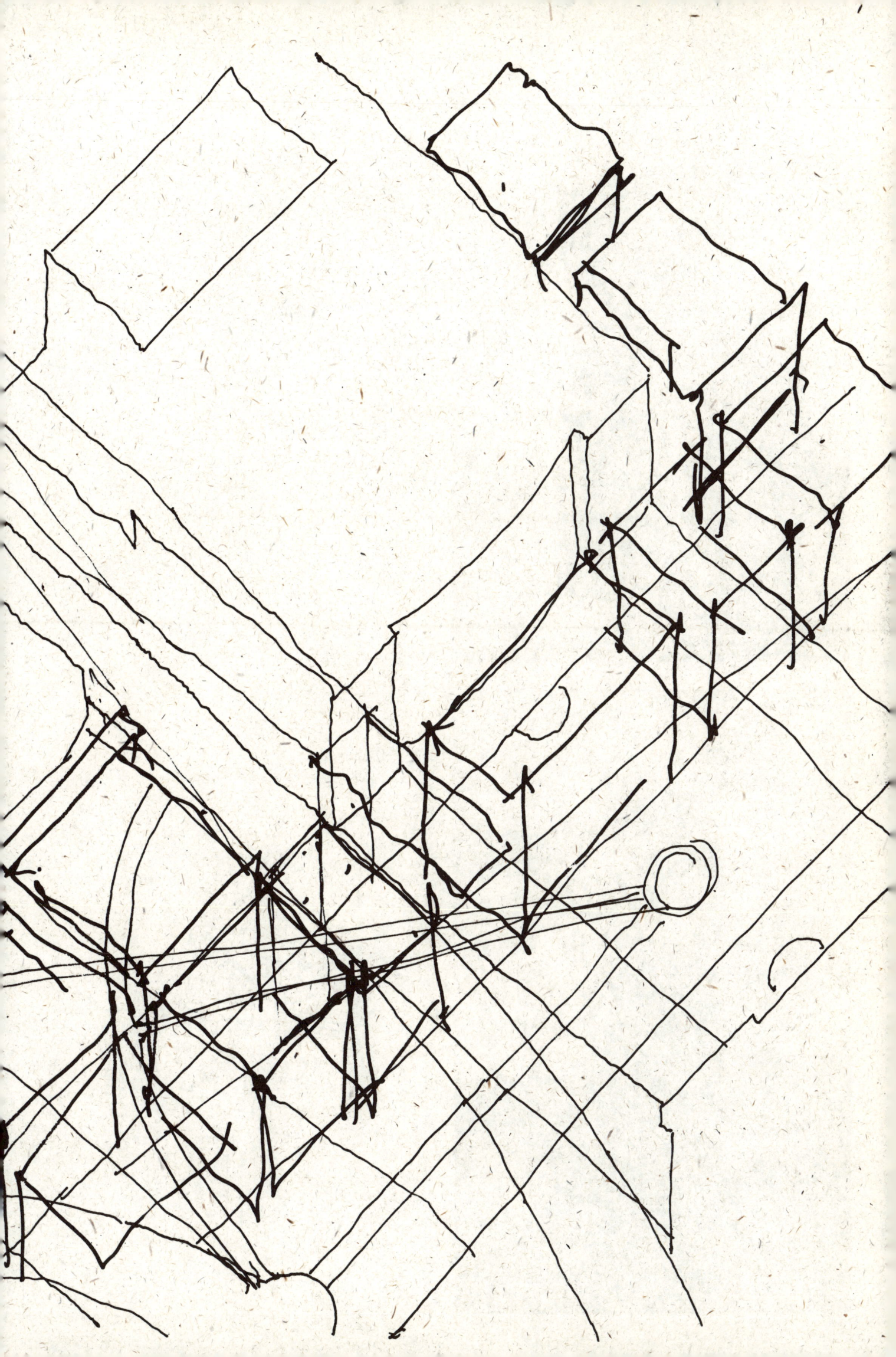

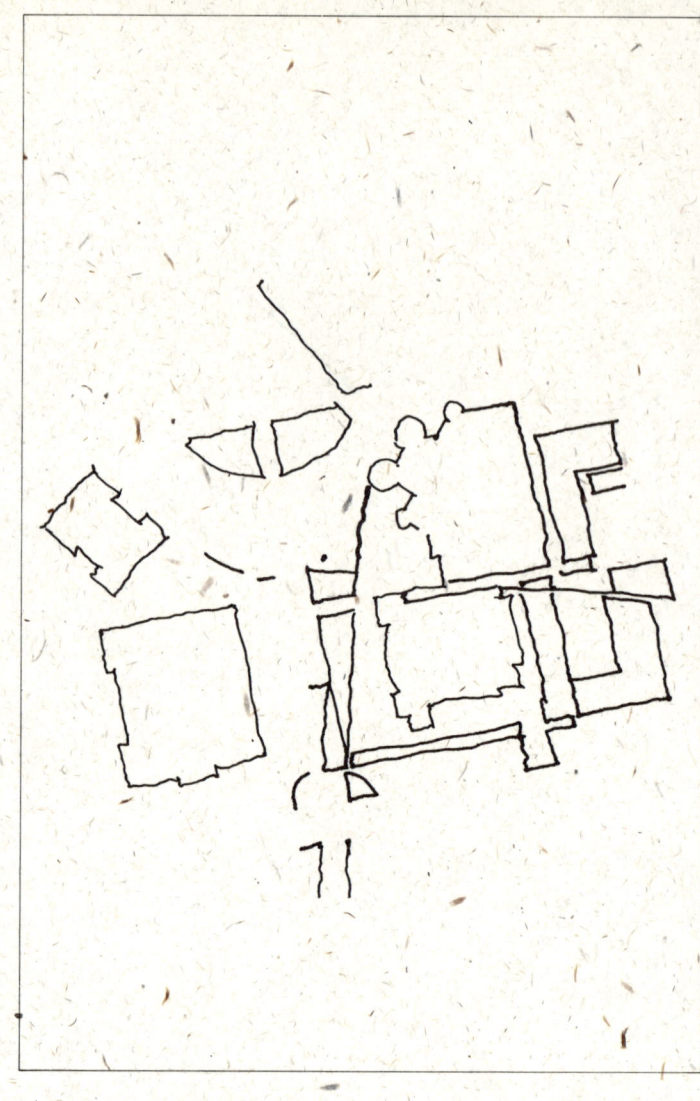

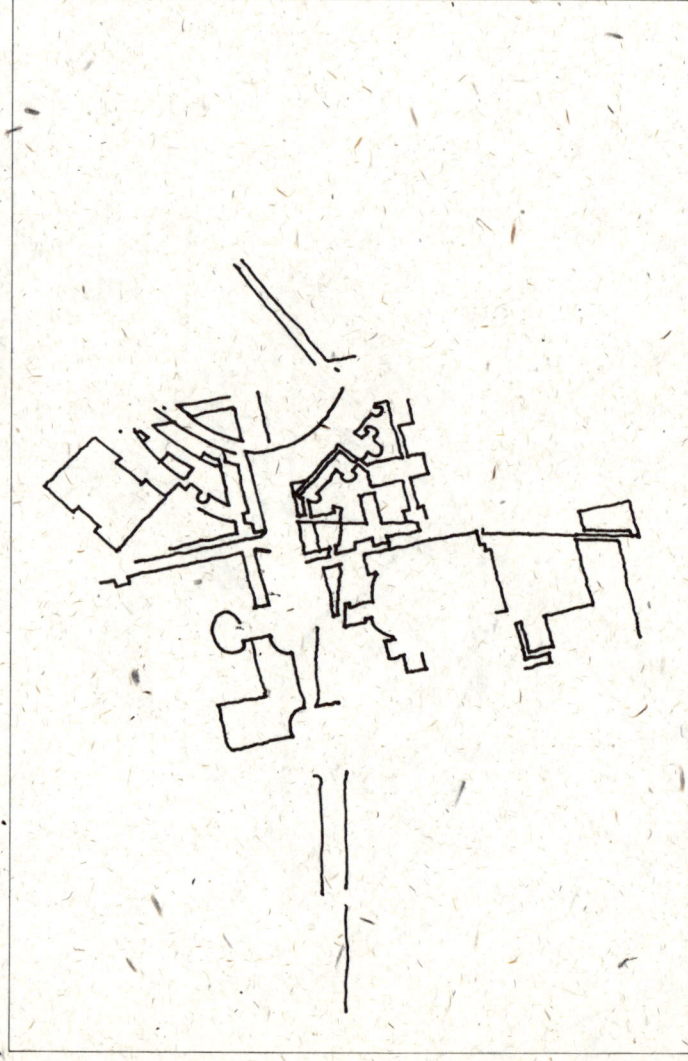

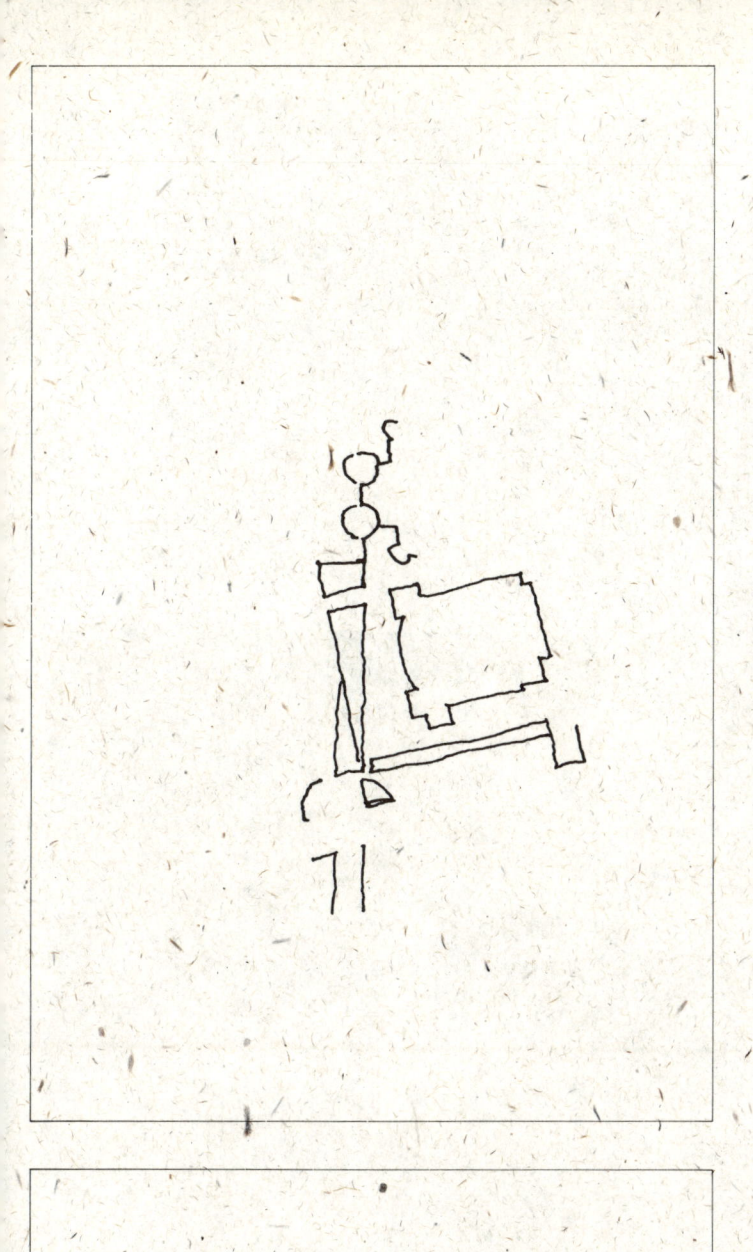
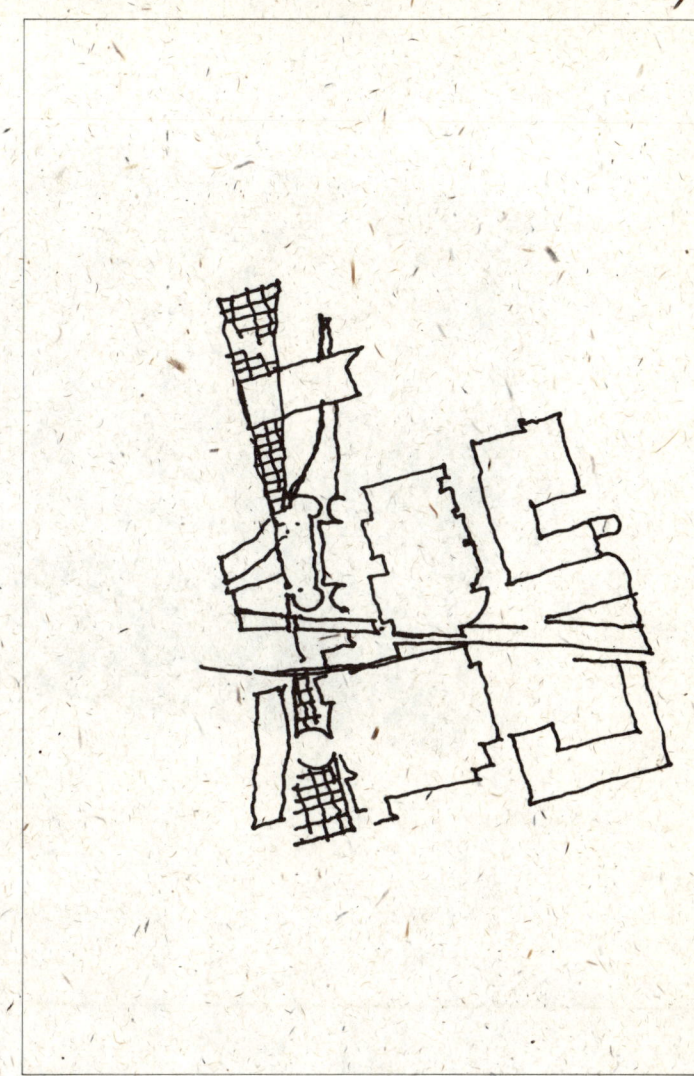
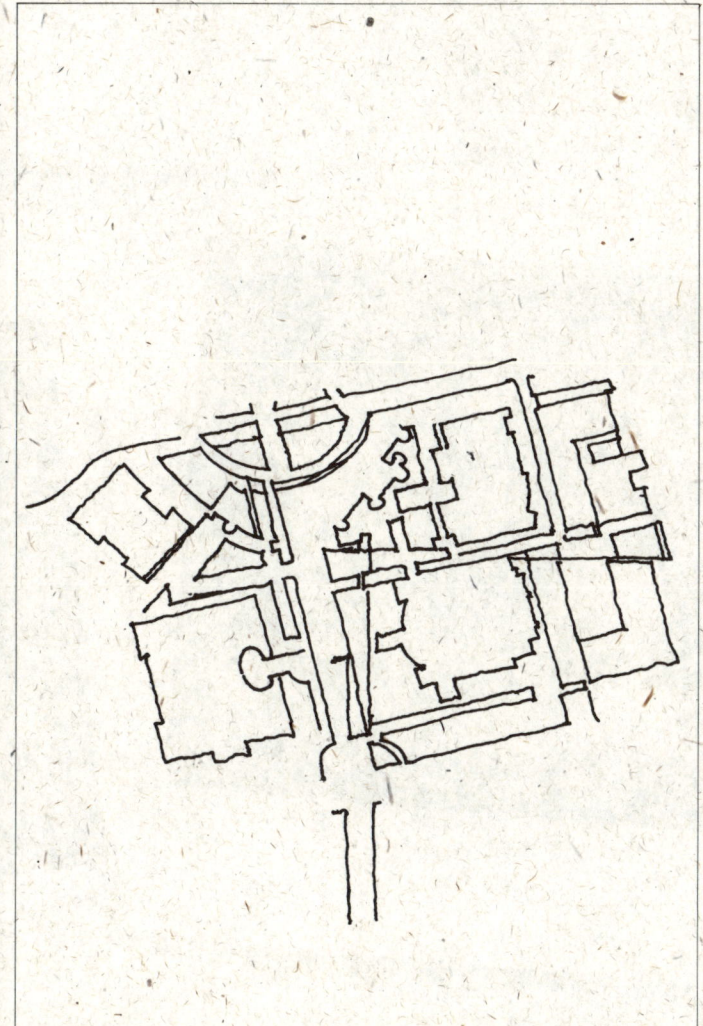
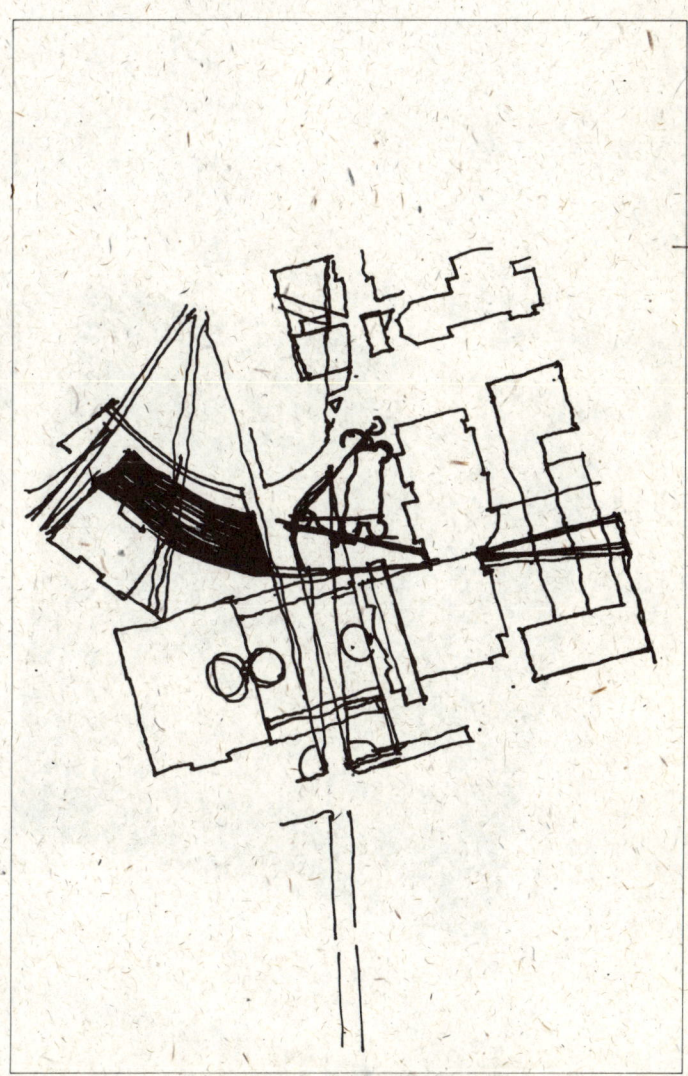

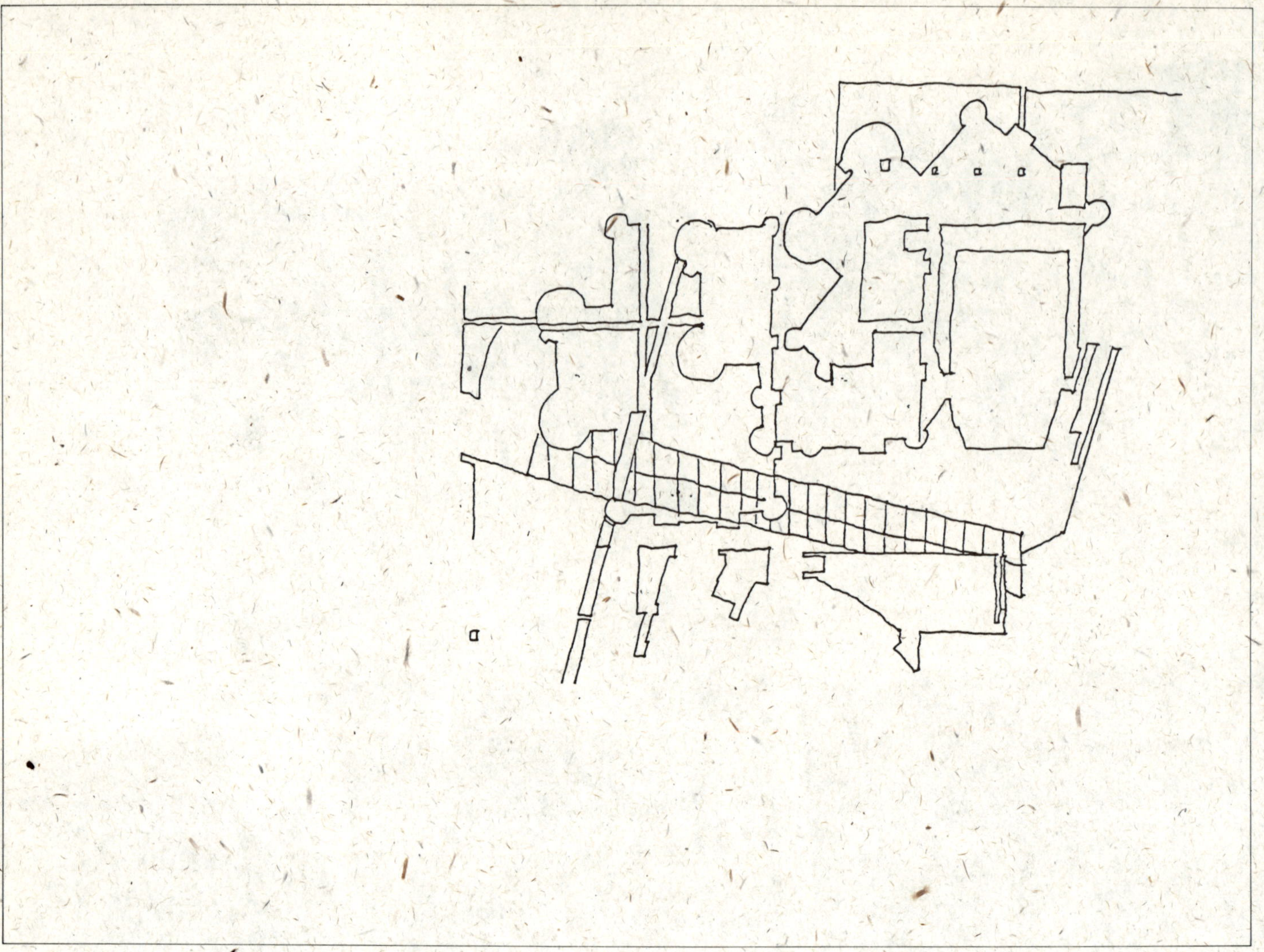

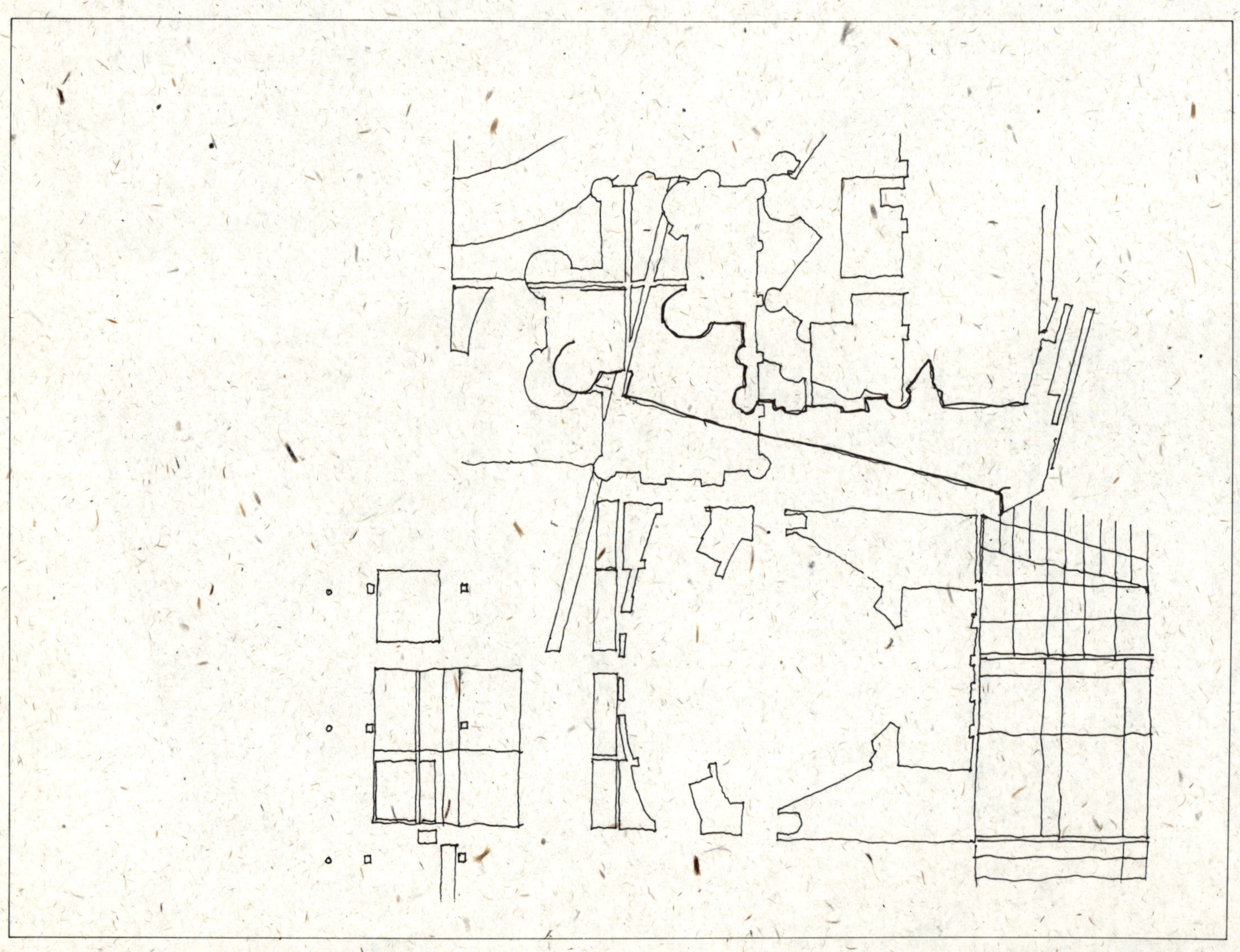

60

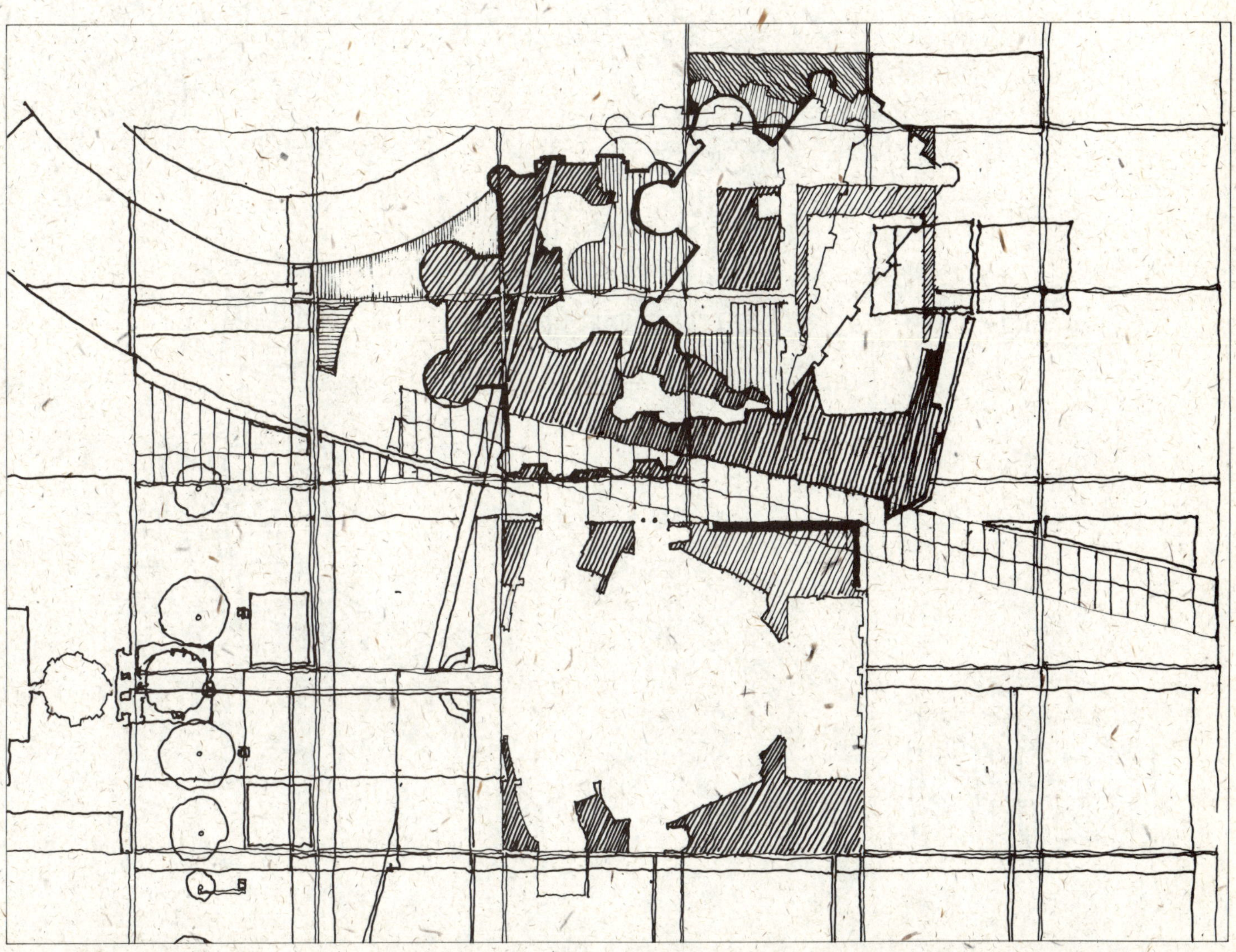

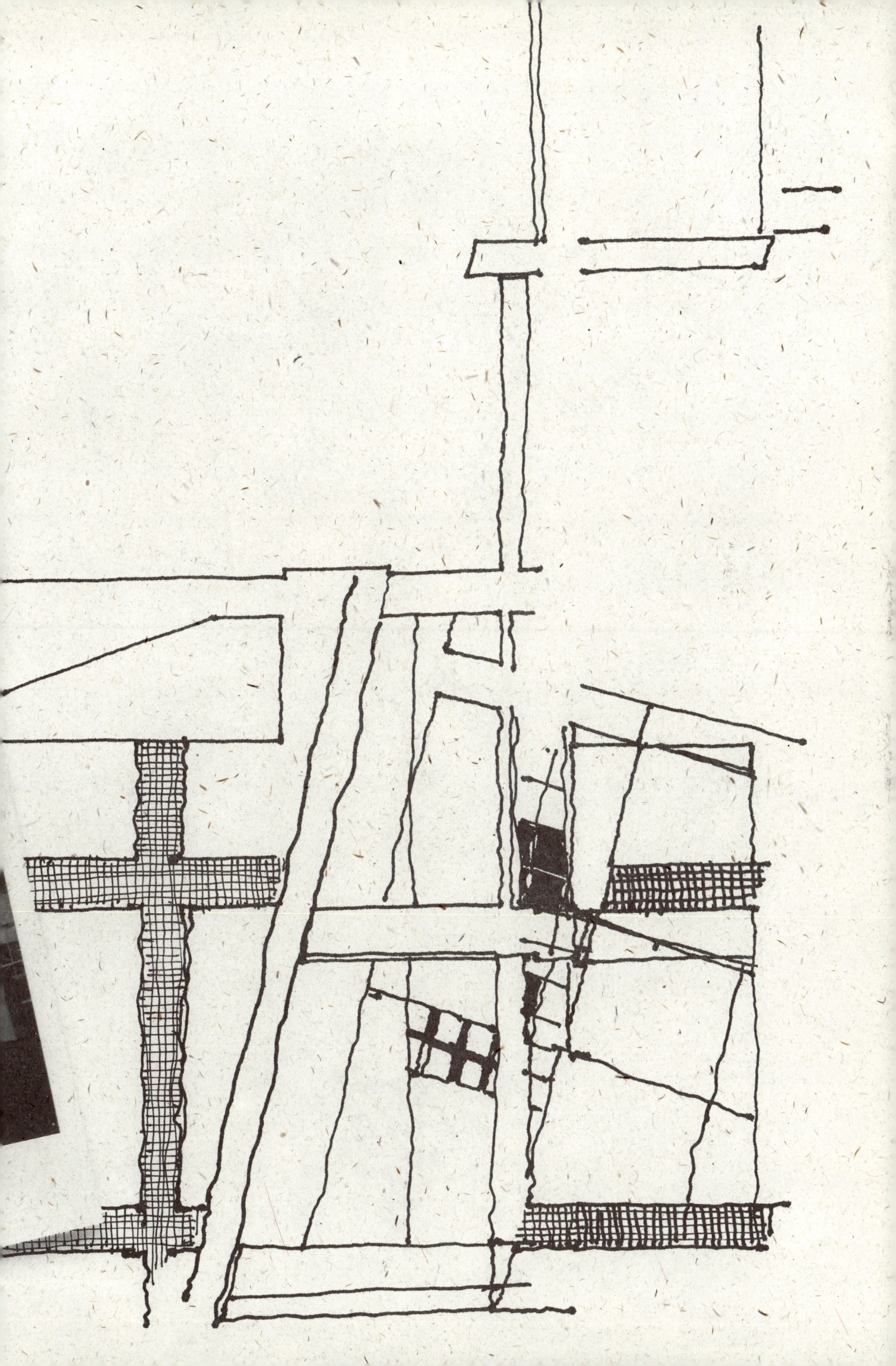

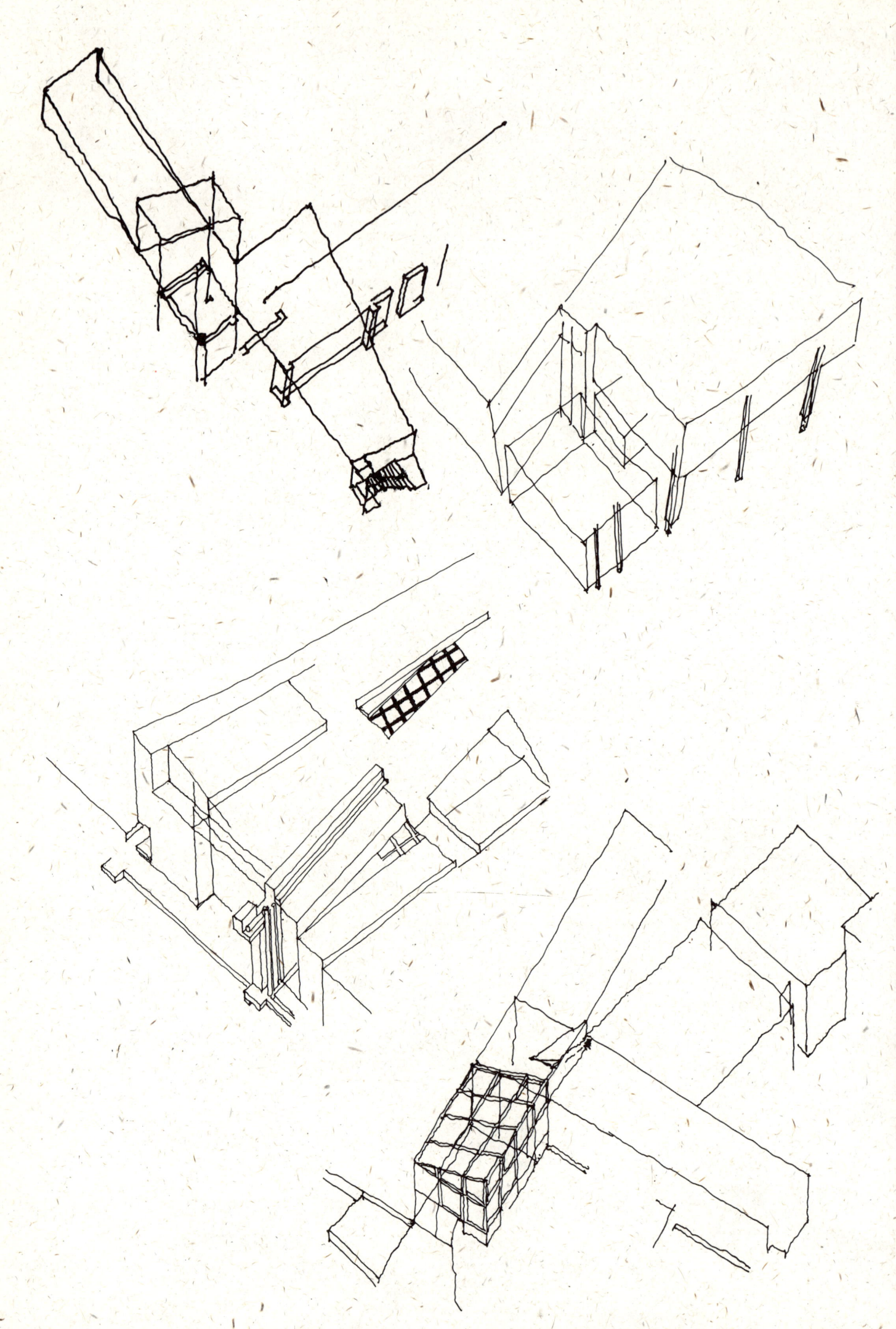

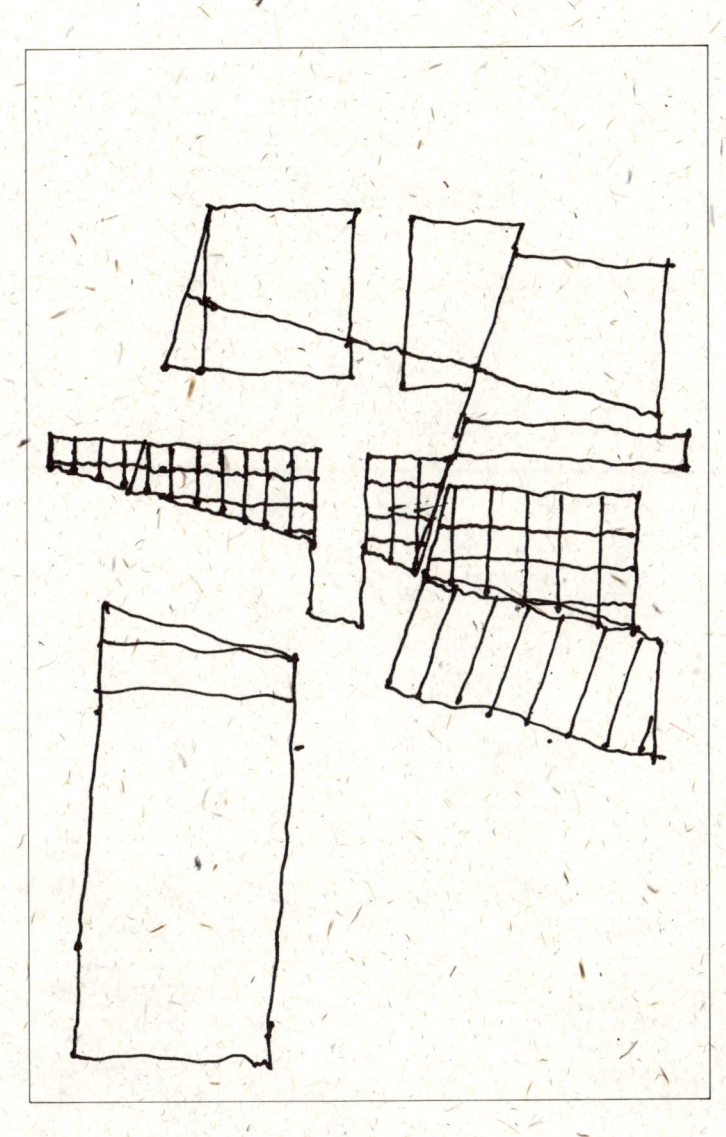

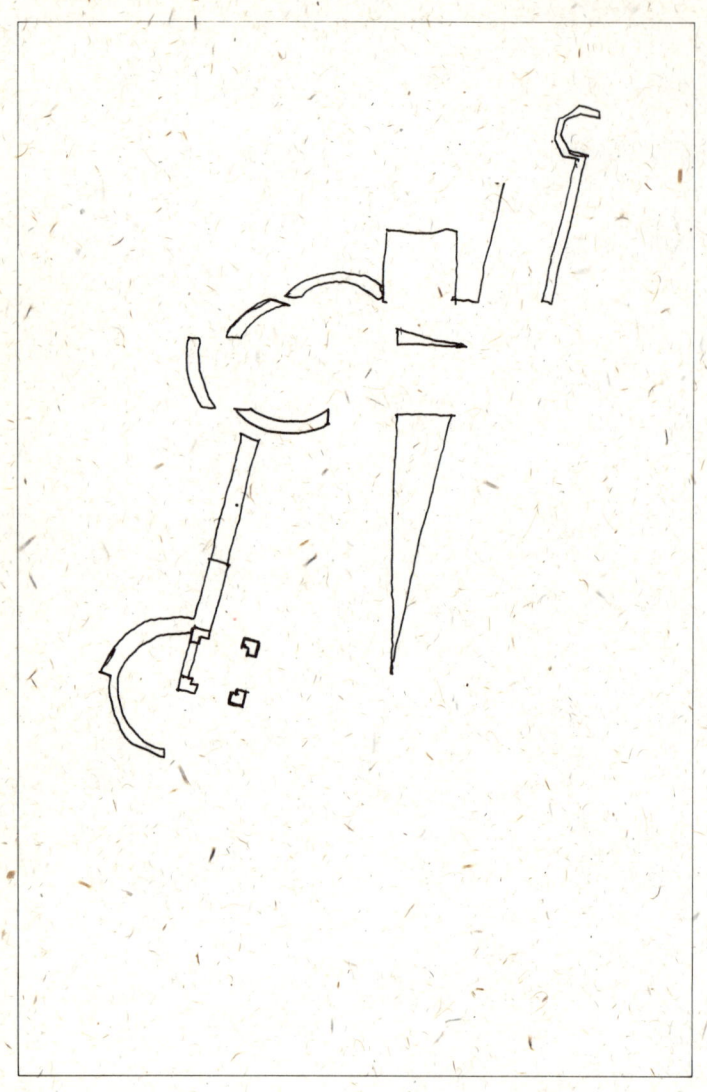
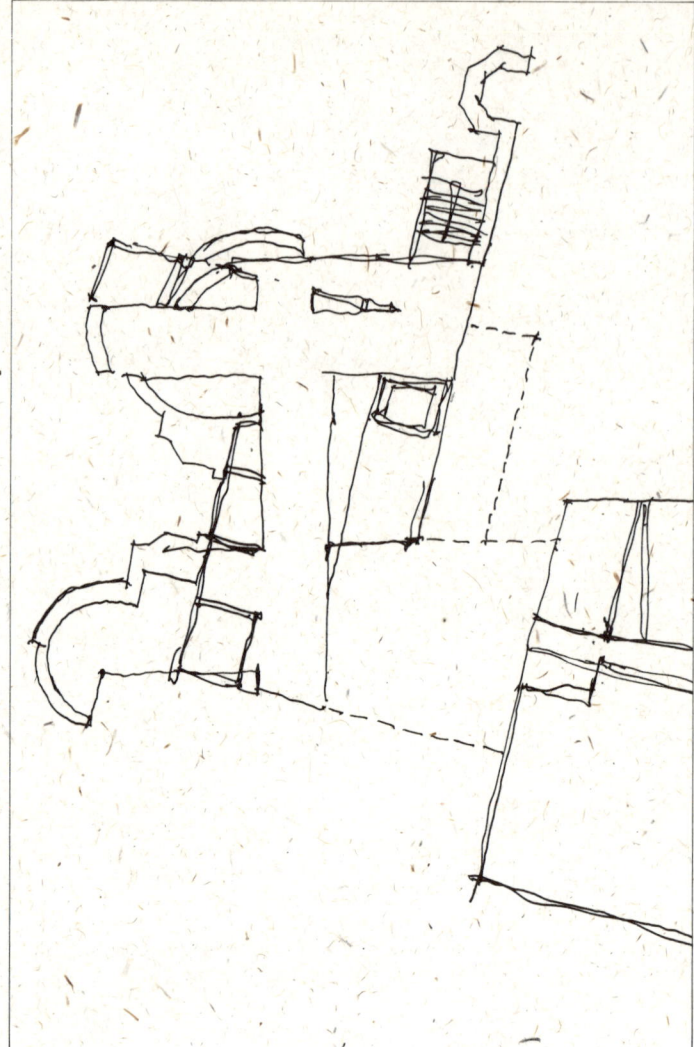
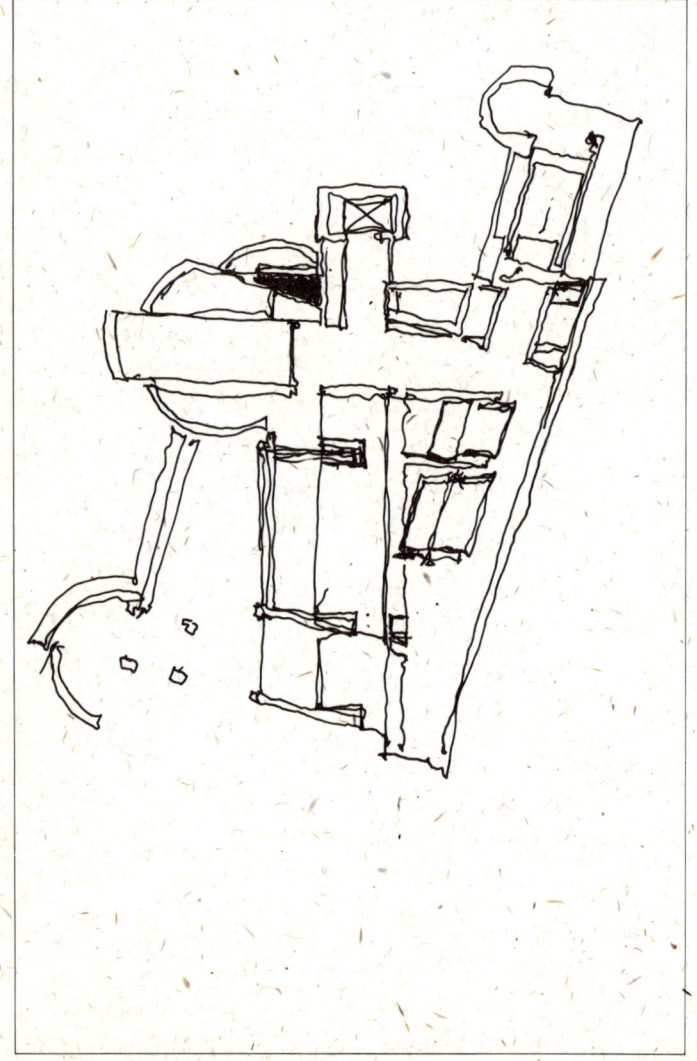
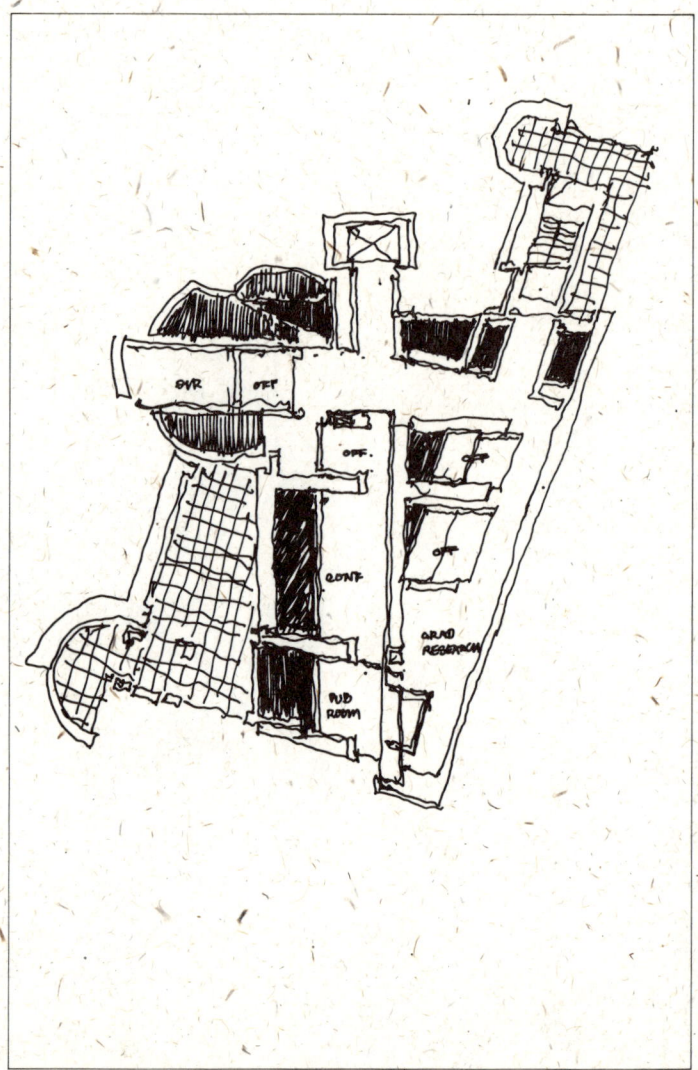

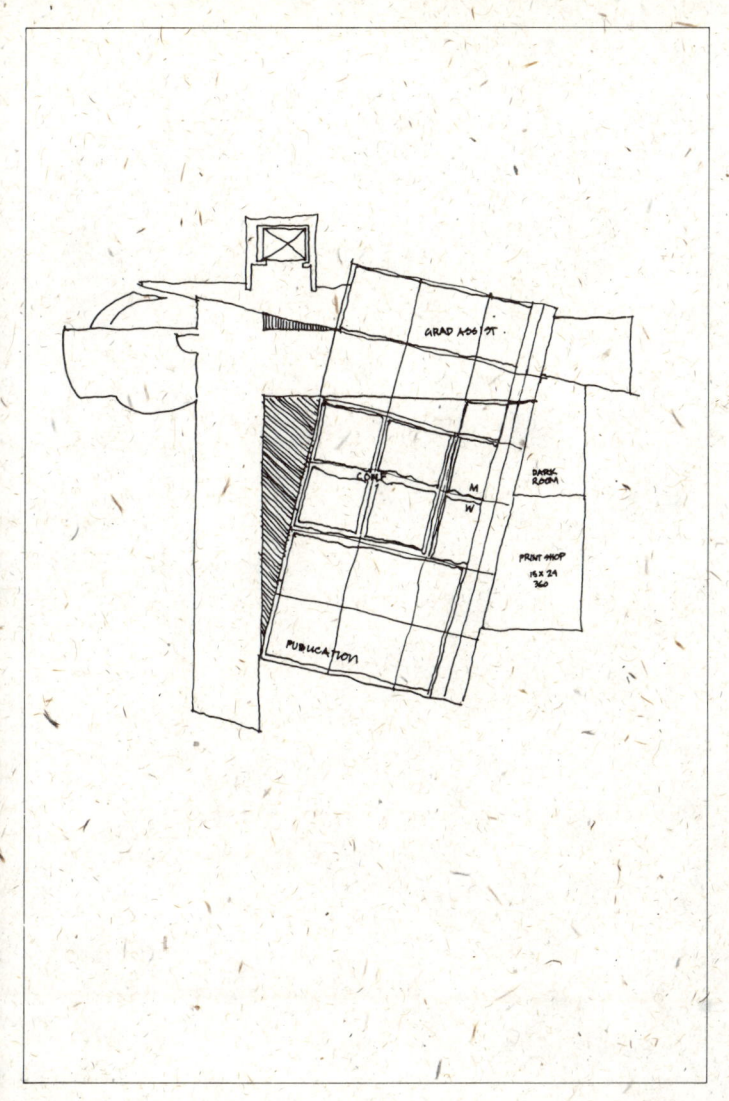

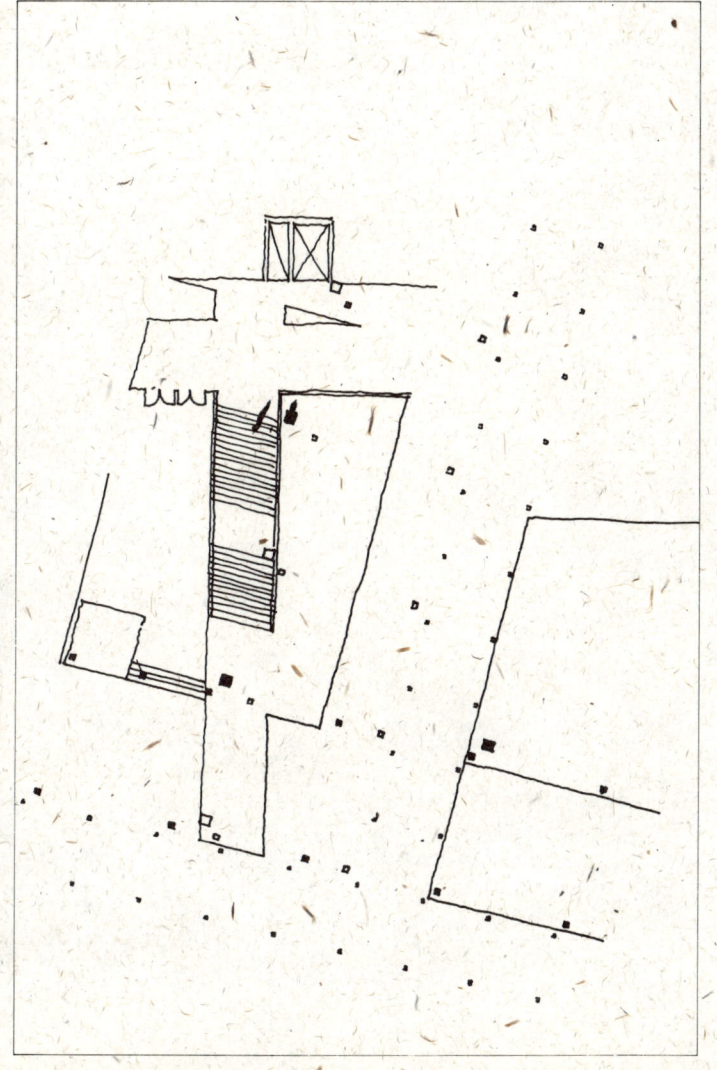
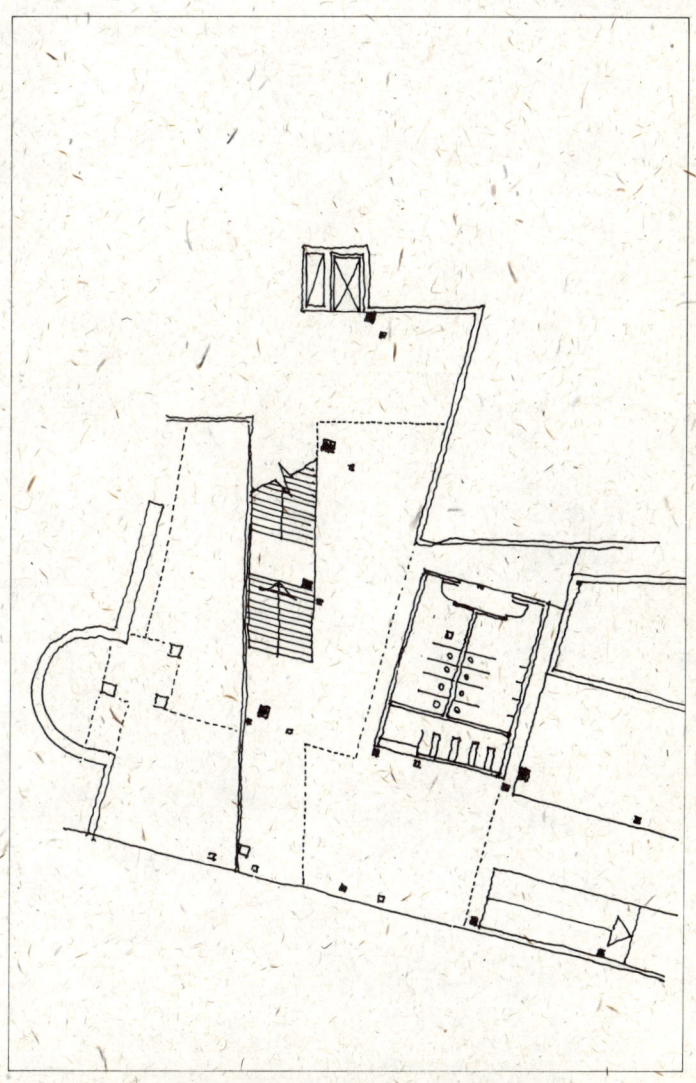

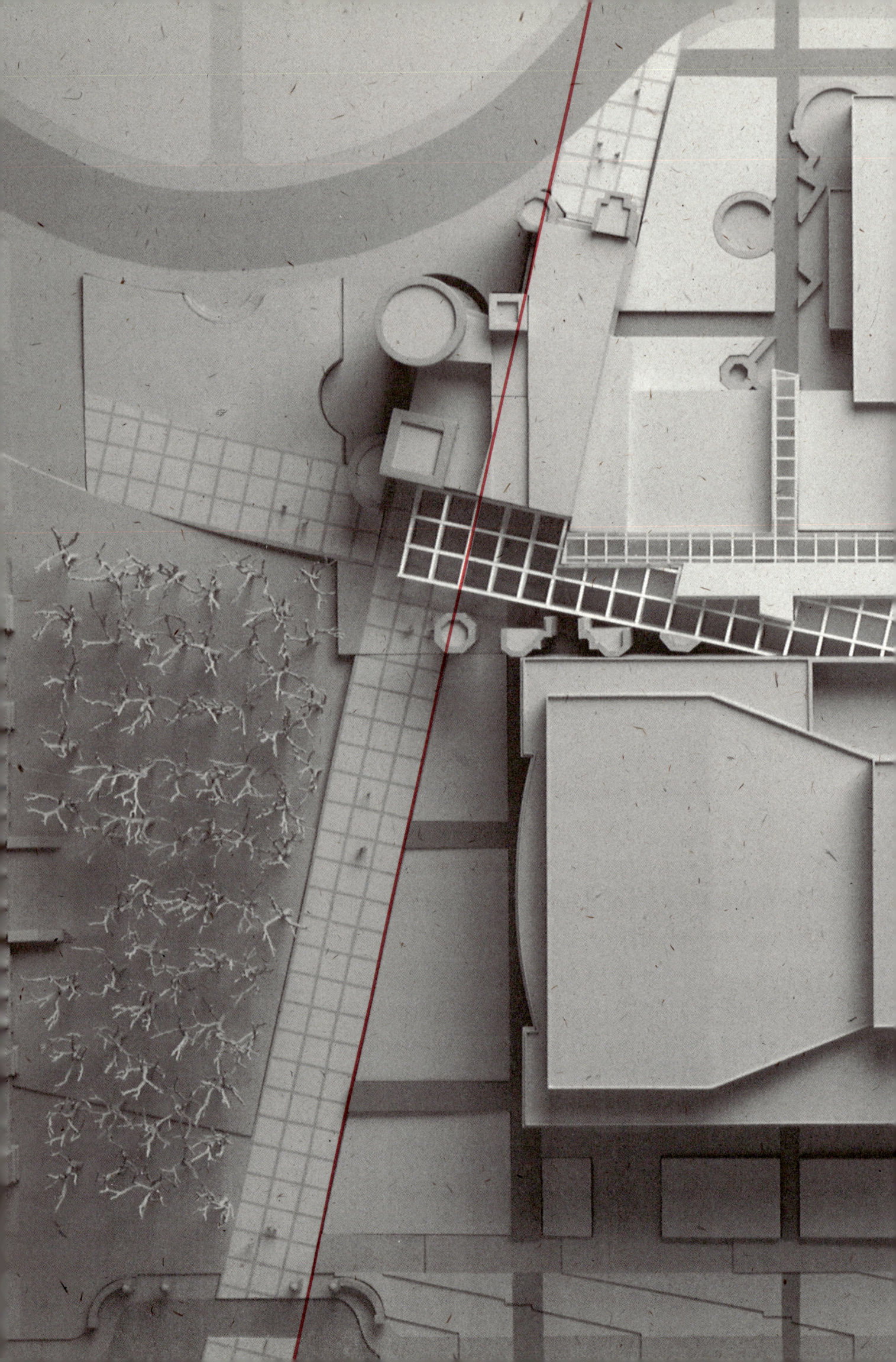

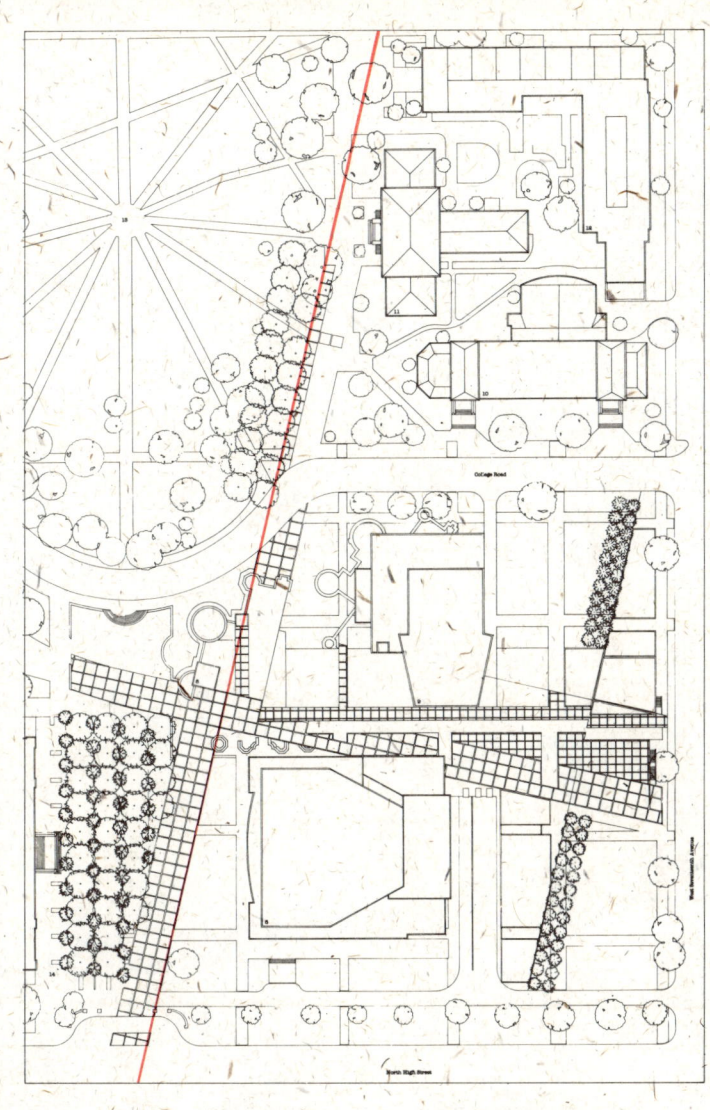
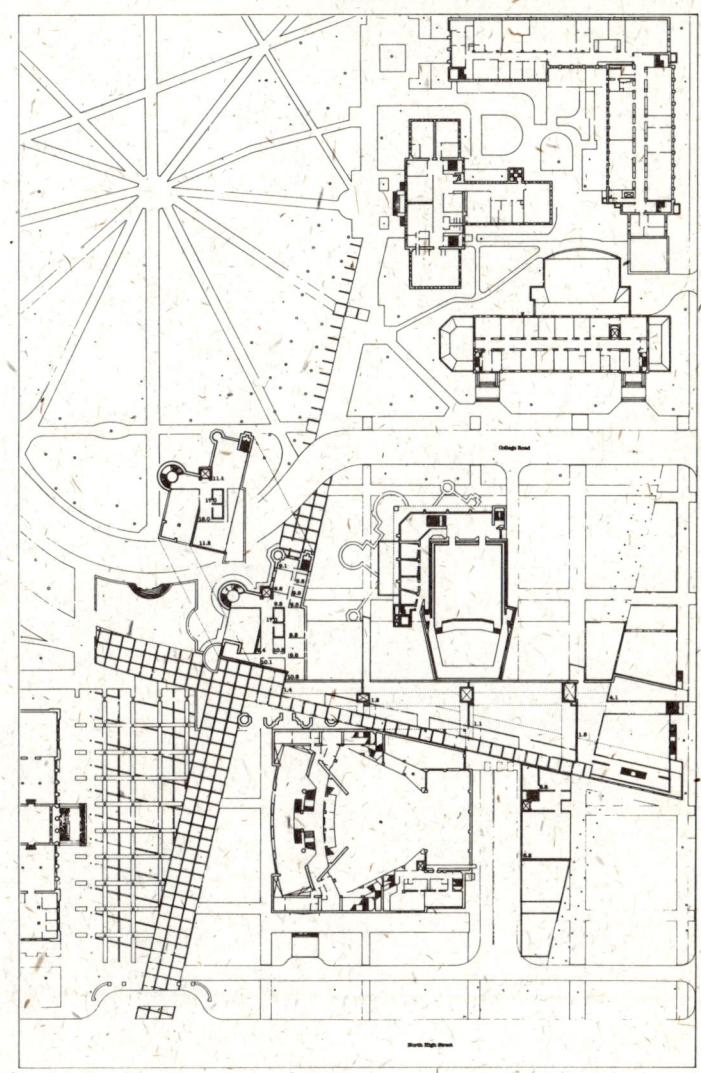
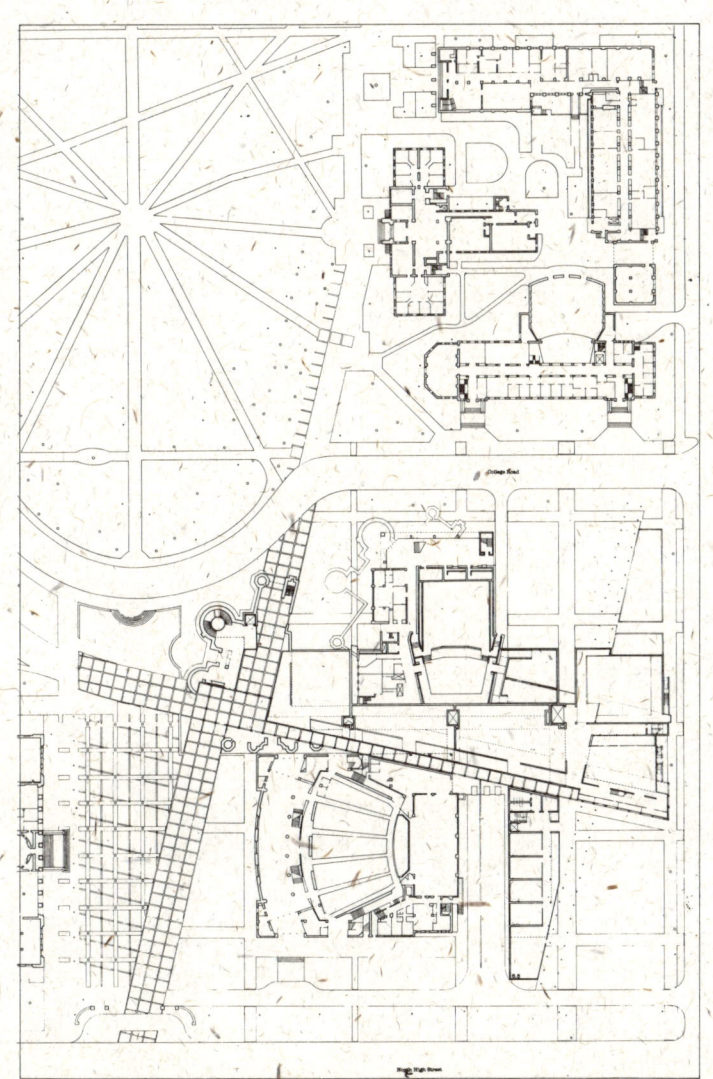
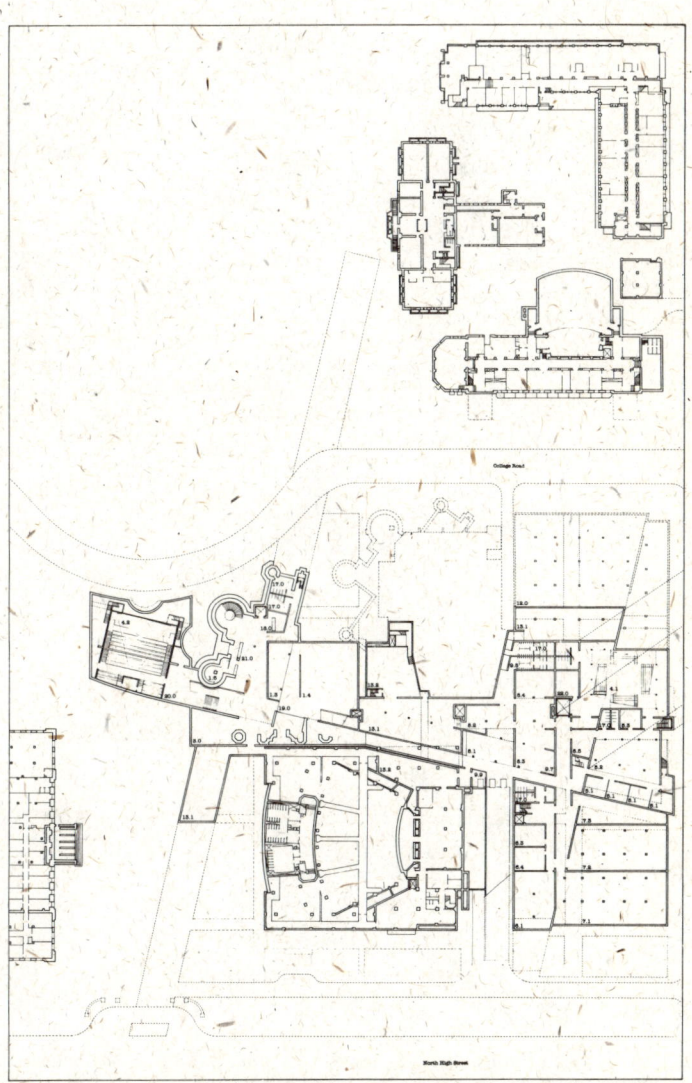

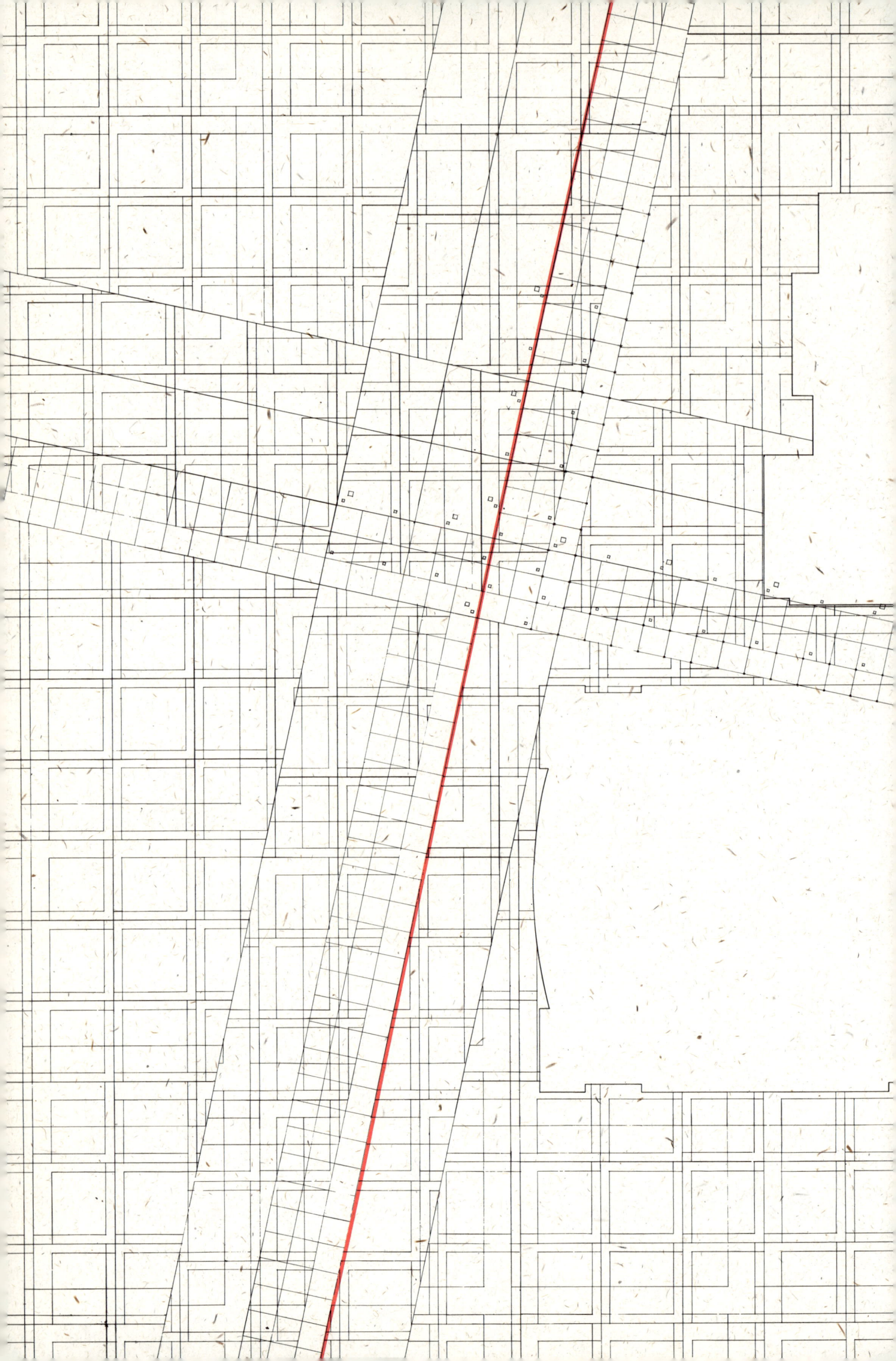

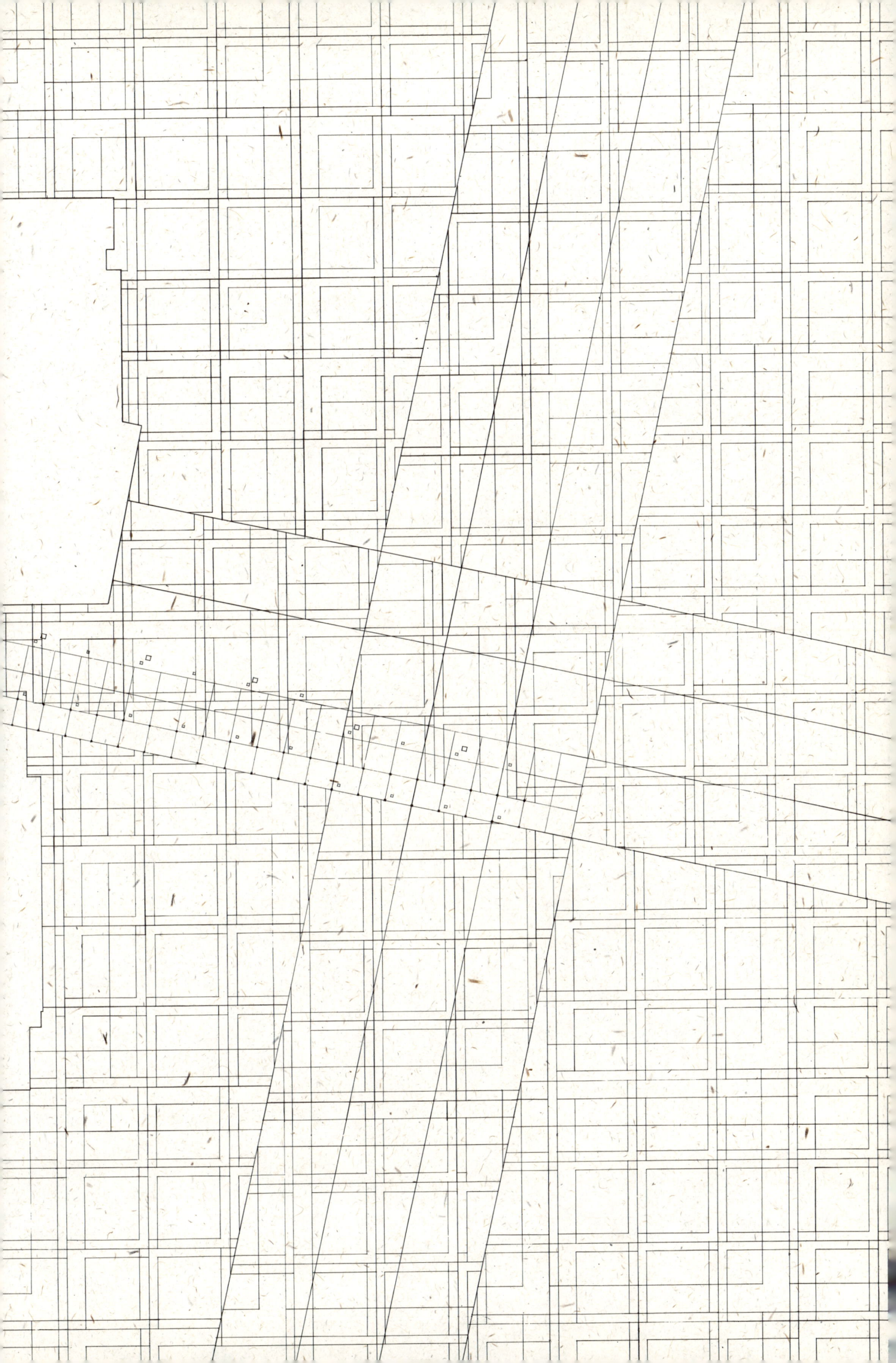

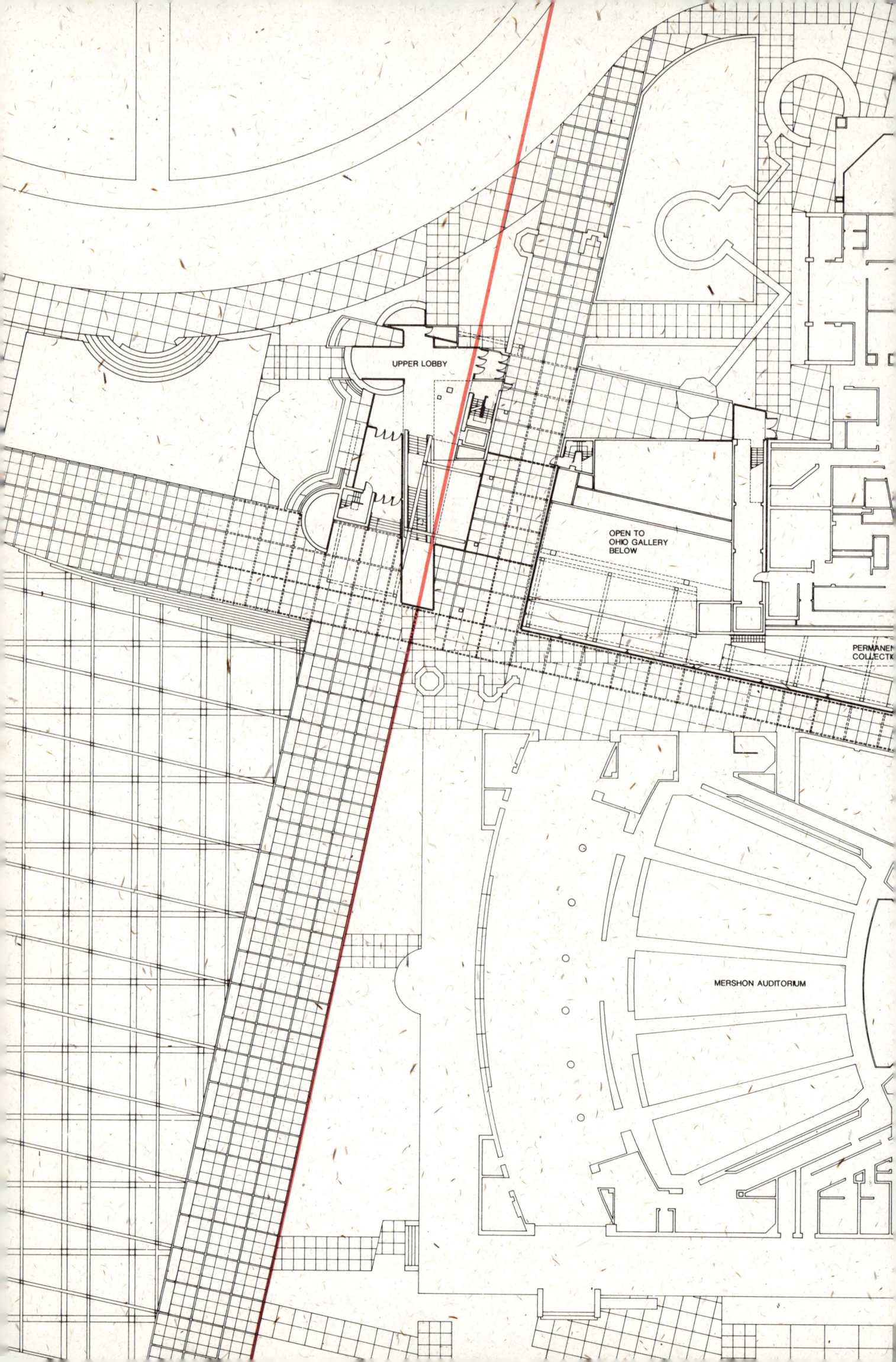

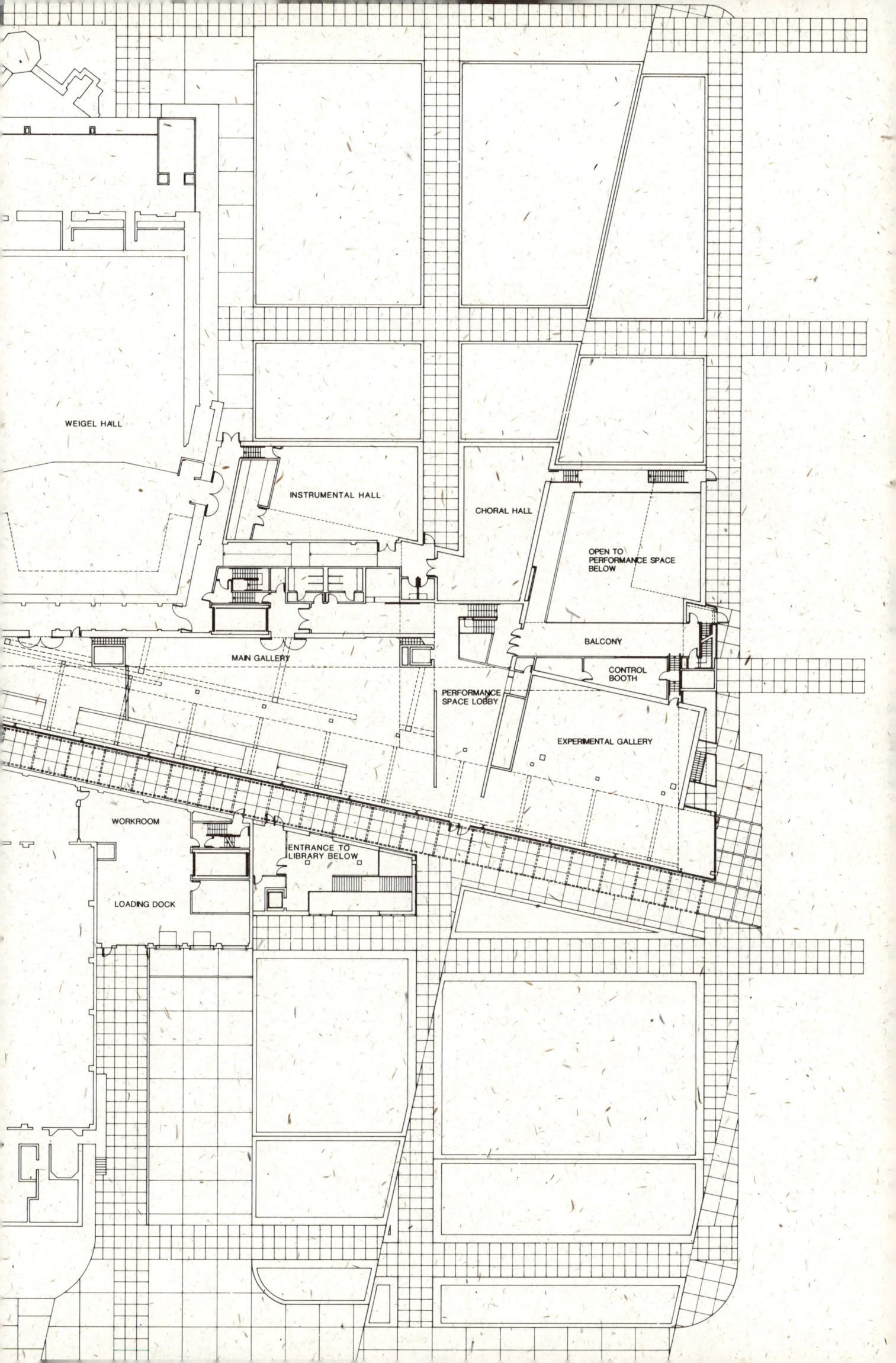

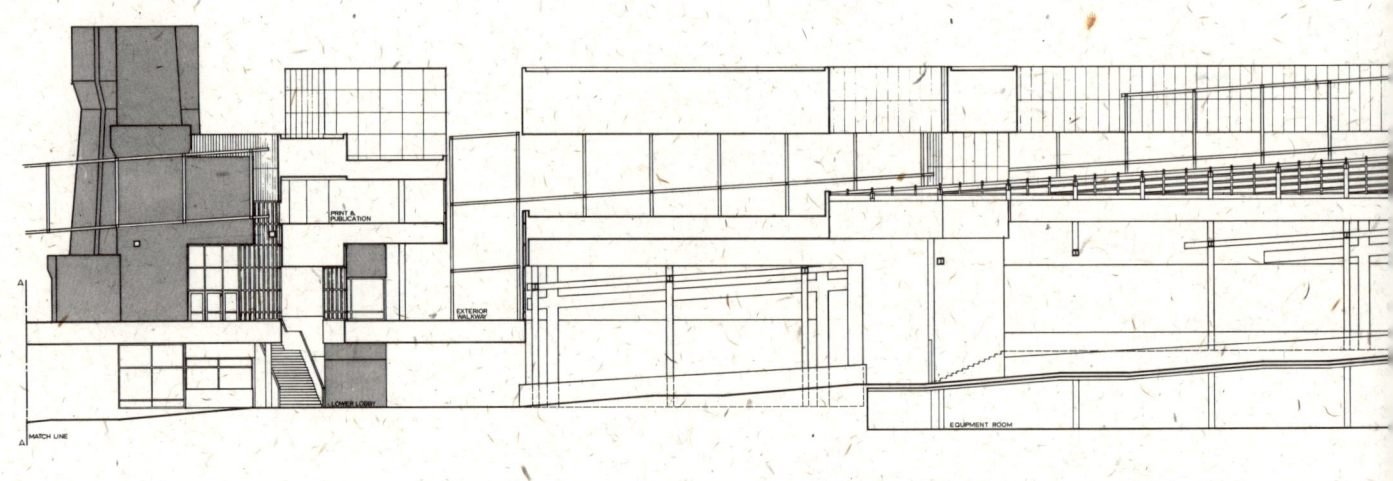

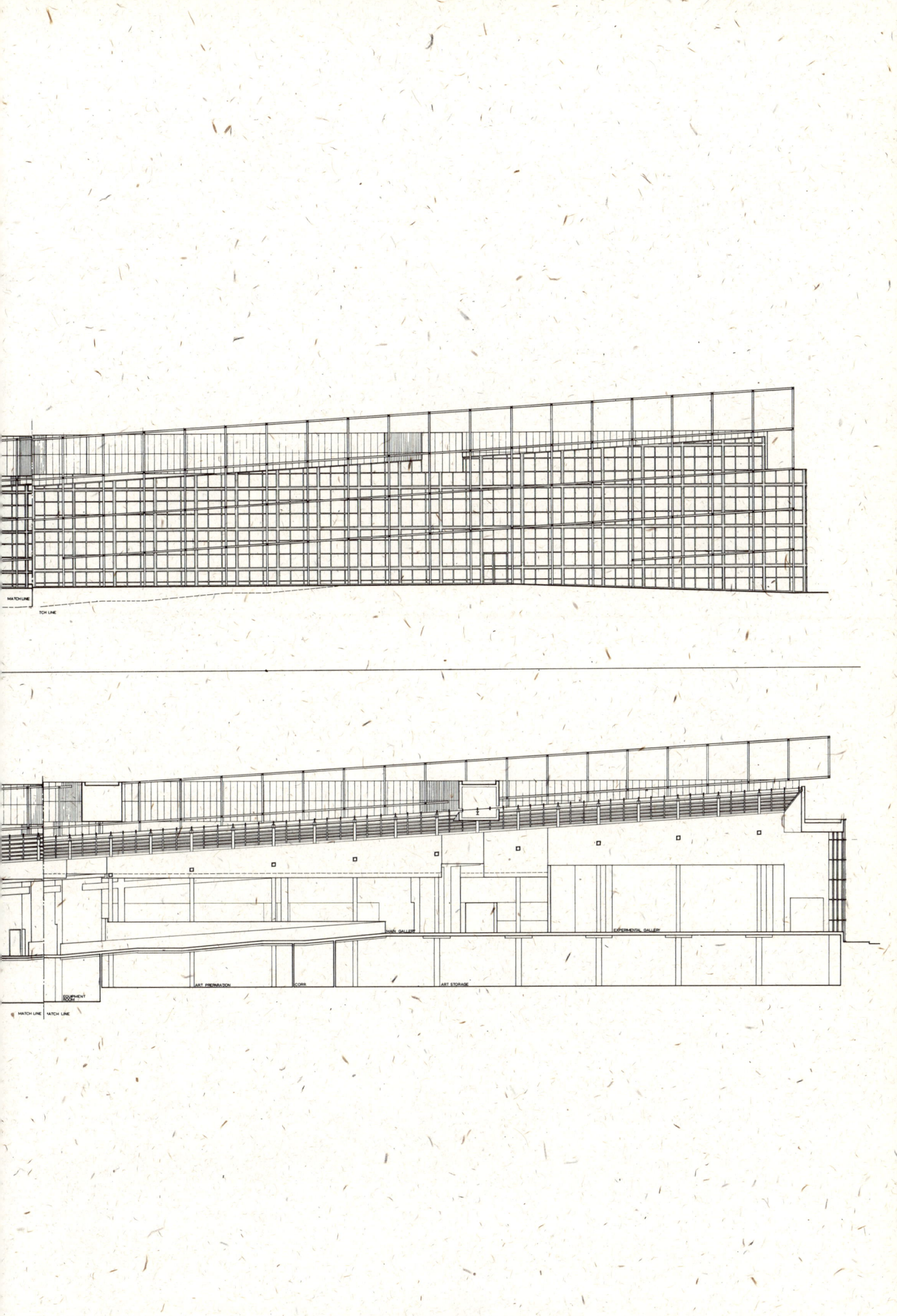

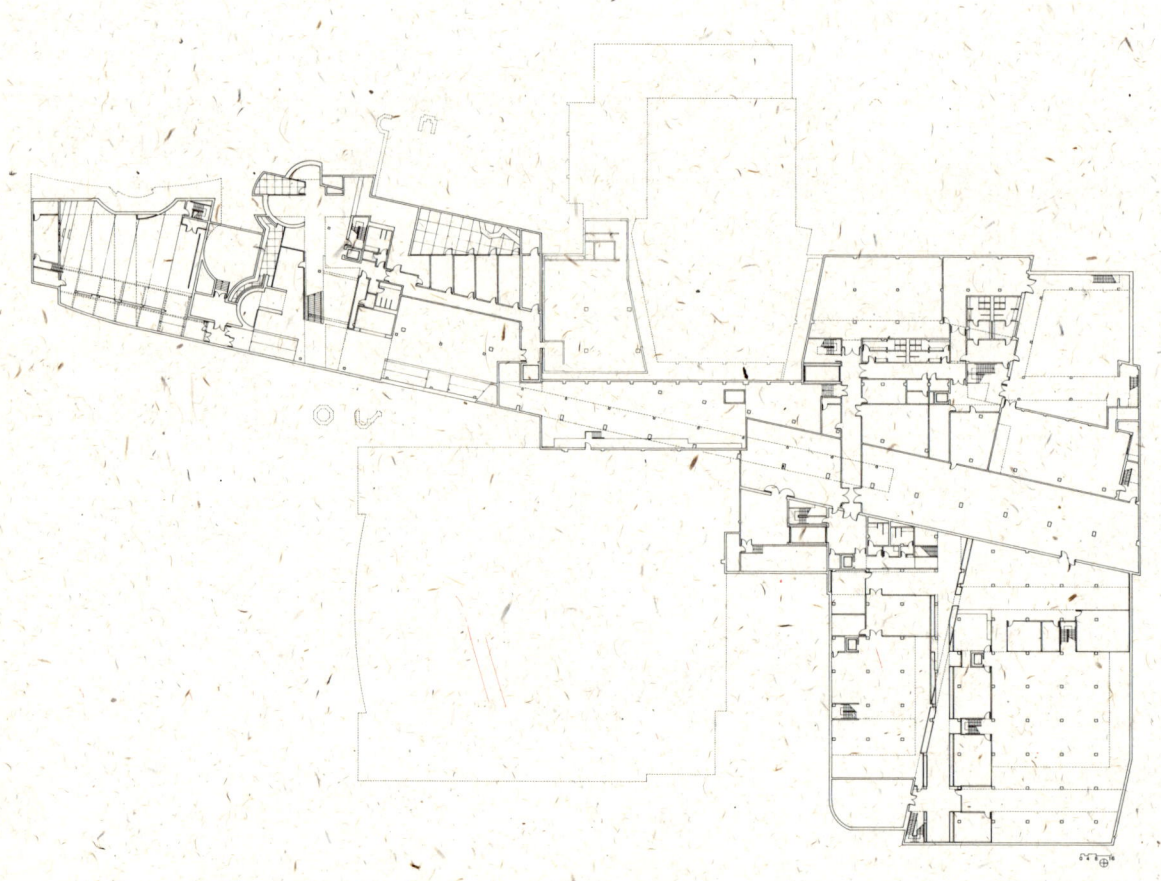

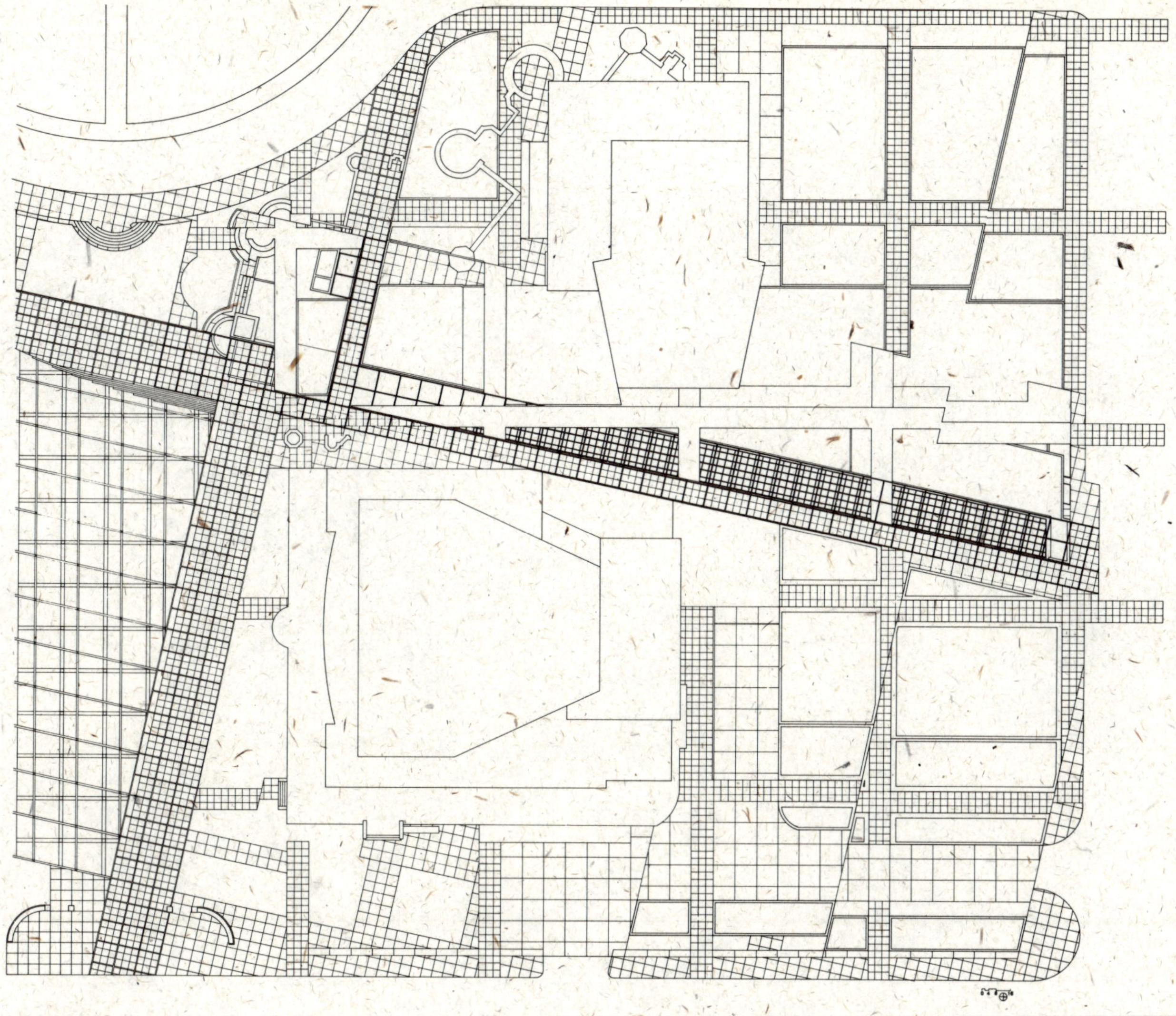

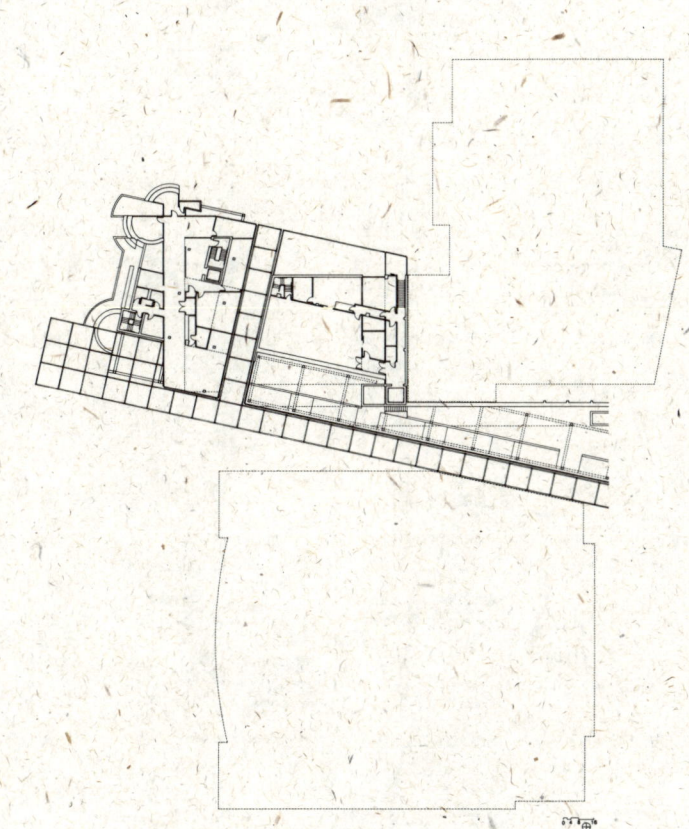

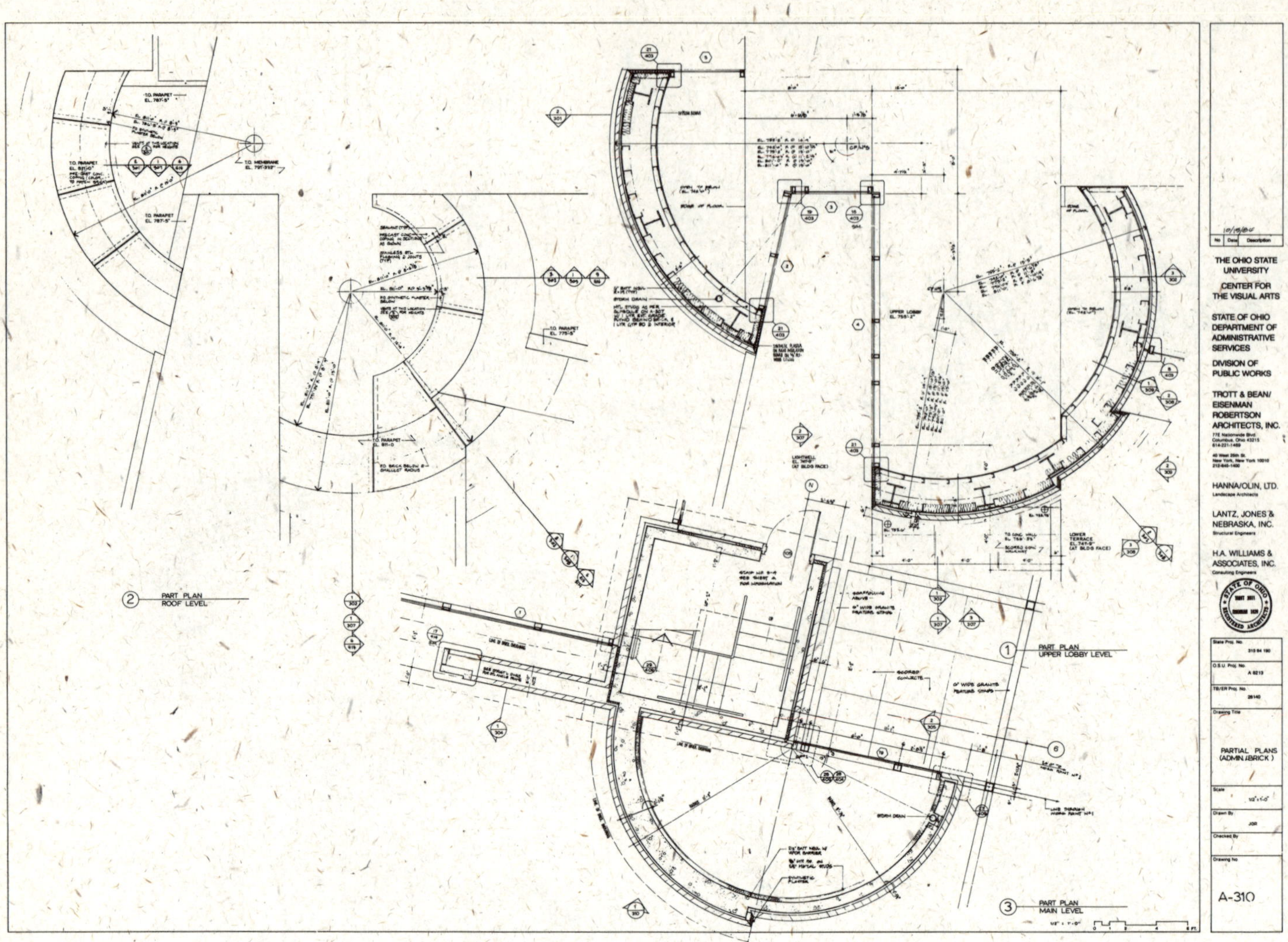

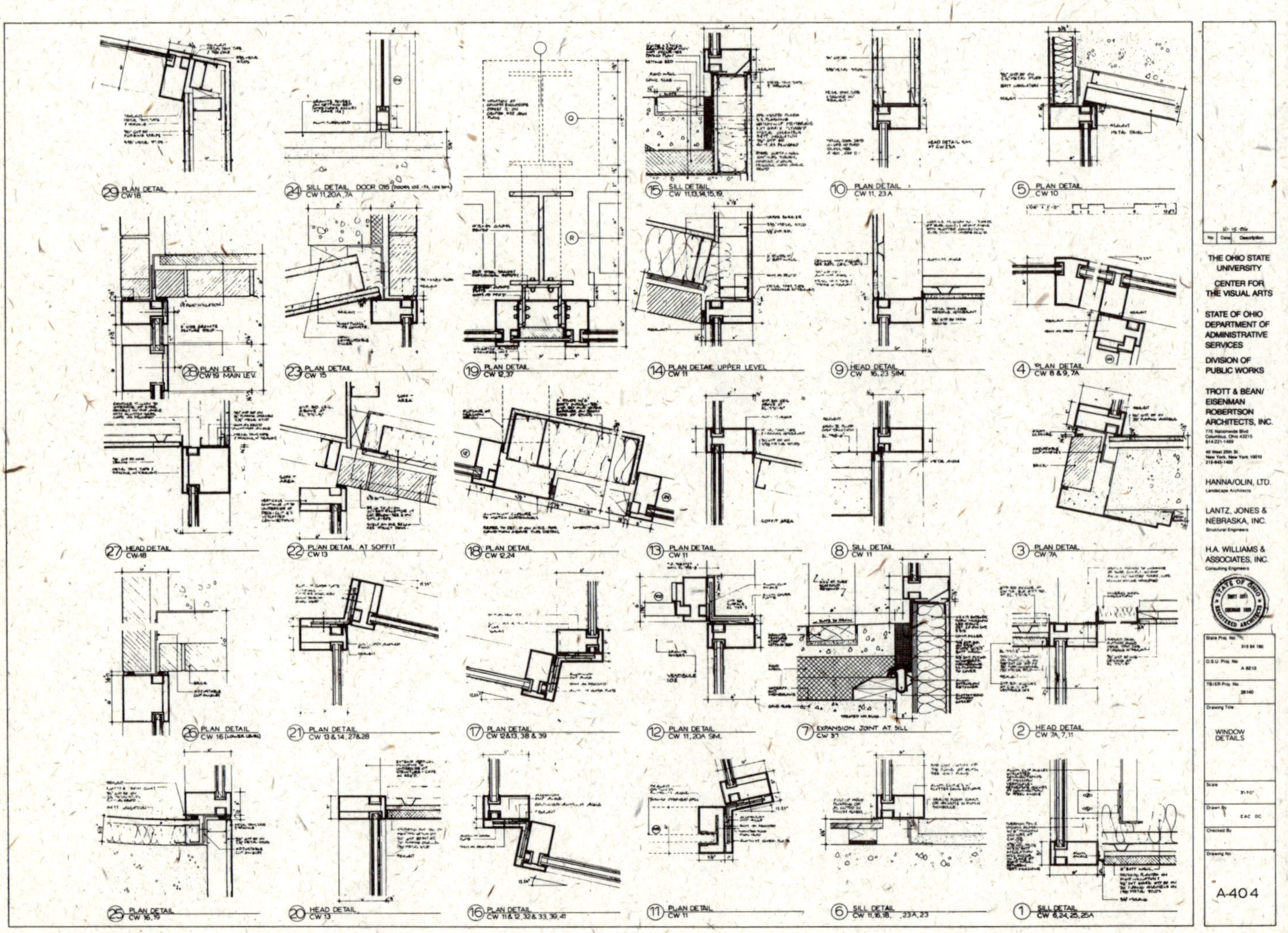

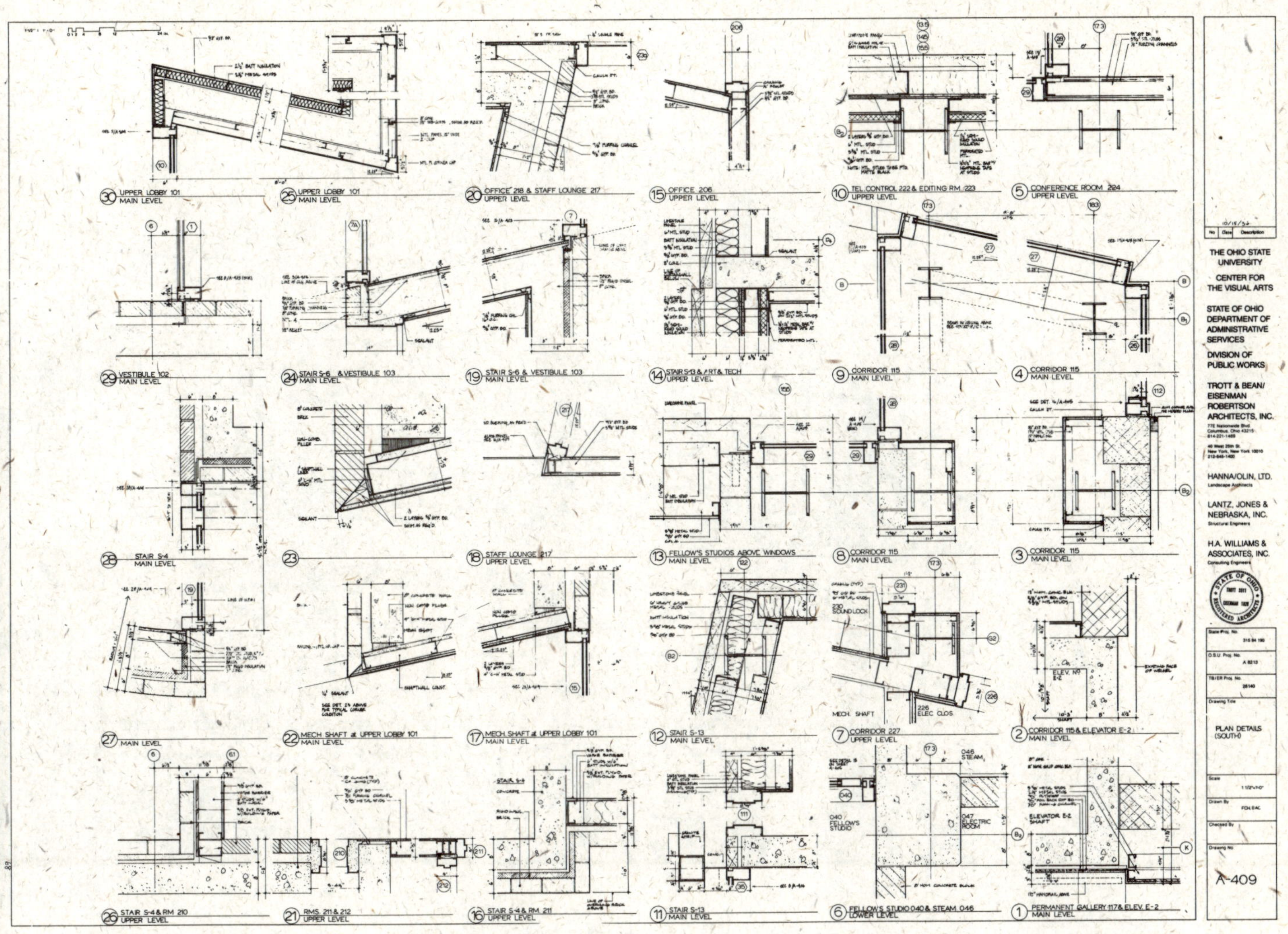
UPPER LOBBY 101 MAIN LEVEL
OFFICE 218 & STAFF LOUNGE 217 UPPER LEVEL
OFFICE 206 UPPER LEVEL
TEL CONTROL 222 & EDITING RM. 223 UPPER LEVEL
CONFERENCE ROOM 224 UPPER LEVEL
VESTIBULE 102 MAIN LEVEL
STAIR S-6 & VESTIBULE 103
STAIR S-6 & VESTIBULE 103
STAIR S-13 & ART & TECH UPPER LEVEL
CORRIDOR 115 MAIN LEVEL
STAIR S-4 MAIN LEVEL
STAFF LOUNGE 217 UPPER LEVEL
FELLOW'S STUDIOS ABOVE WINDOWS MAIN LEVEL
MAIN LEVEL
MECH SHAFT at UPPER LOBBY 101 MAIN LEVEL
MECH SHAFT at UPPER LOBBY 101 MAIN LEVEL
STAIR S-13 MAIN LEVEL
CORRIDOR 227 UPPER LEVEL
CORRIDOR 115 & ELEVATOR E-2 MAIN LEVEL
STAIR S-4 & RM 210 UPPER LEVEL
RMS. 211 & 212 UPPER LEVEL
STAIR S-4 & RM 211 UPPER LEVEL
FELLOW'S STUDIO 040 & STEAM 046 LOWER LEVEL
PERMANENT GALLERY 117 & ELEV. E-2 MAIN LEVEL
THE OHIO STATE UNIVERSITY
CENTER FOR THE VISUAL ARTS
STATE OF OHIO DEPARTMENT OF ADMINISTRATIVE SERVICES
DIVISION OF PUBLIC WORKS
TROTT & BEAN/ EISENMAN ROBERTSON ARCHITECTS, INC.
HANNA/OLIN, LTD.
LANTZ, JONES & NEBRASKA, INC.
H.A. WILLIAMS & ASSOCIATES, INC.
PLAN DETAILS (SOUTH)
A-409

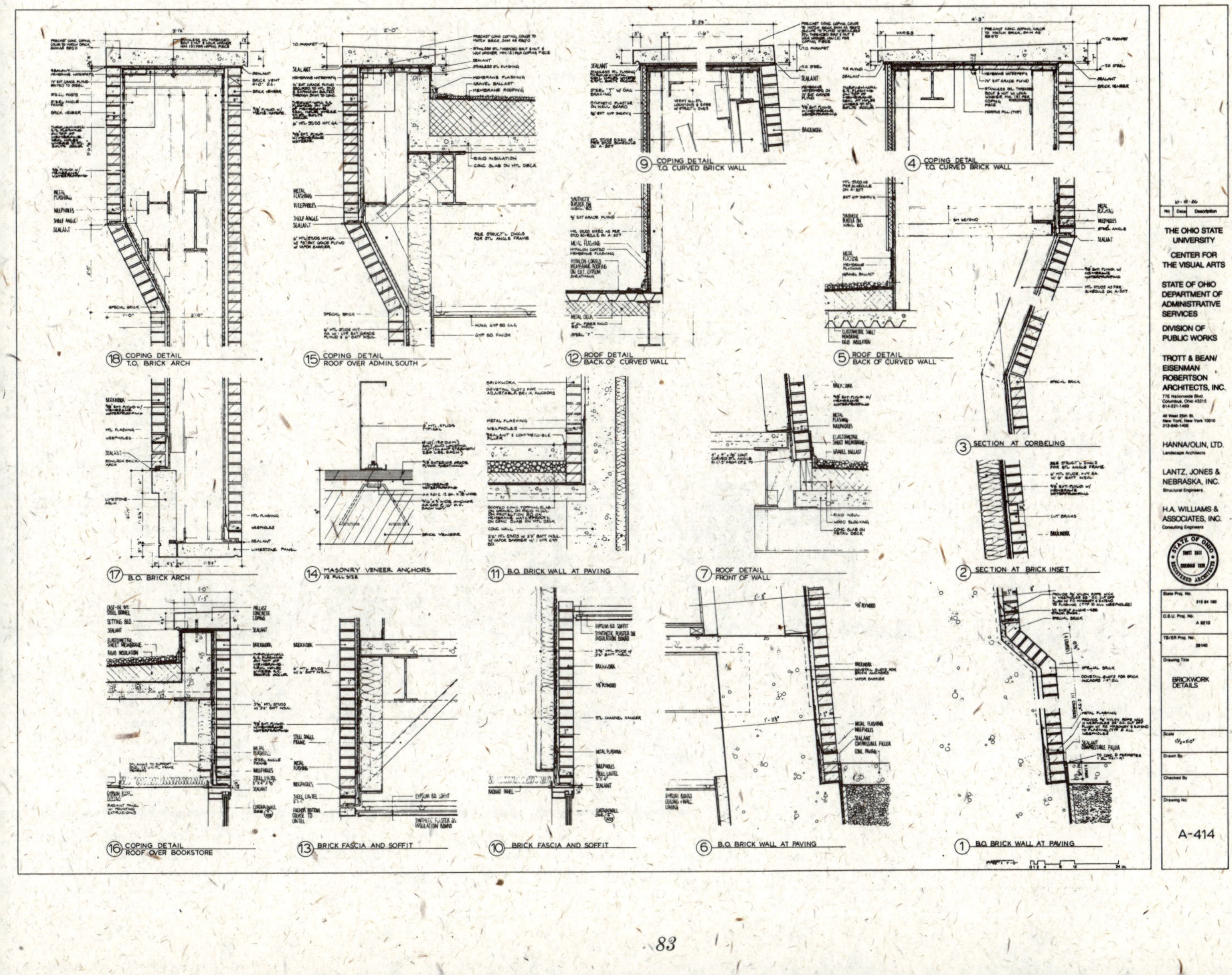
COPING DETAIL T.O. CURVED BRICK WALL
COPING DETAIL T.O. CURVED BRICK WALL
COPING DETAIL T.O. BRICK ARCH
COPING DETAIL ROOF OVER ADMIN. SOUTH
ROOF DETAIL BACK OF CURVED WALL
ROOF DETAIL BACK OF CURVED WALL
SECTION AT CORBELING
B.O. BRICK ARCH
MASONRY VENEER ANCHORS
B.O. BRICK WALL AT PAVING
ROOF DETAIL FRONT OF WALL
SECTION AT BRICK INSET
COPING DETAIL ROOF OVER BOOKSTORE
BRICK FASCIA AND SOFFIT
BRICK FASCIA AND SOFFIT
B.O. BRICK WALL AT PAVING
B.O. BRICK WALL AT PAVING
THE OHIO STATE UNIVERSITY
CENTER FOR THE VISUAL ARTS
STATE OF OHIO DEPARTMENT OF ADMINISTRATIVE SERVICES
DIVISION OF PUBLIC WORKS
TROTT & BEAN/ EISENMAN ROBERTSON ARCHITECTS, INC.
HANNA/OLIN, LTD.
LANTZ, JONES & NEBRASKA, INC.
H.A. WILLIAMS & ASSOCIATES, INC.
BRICKWORK DETAILS
A-414

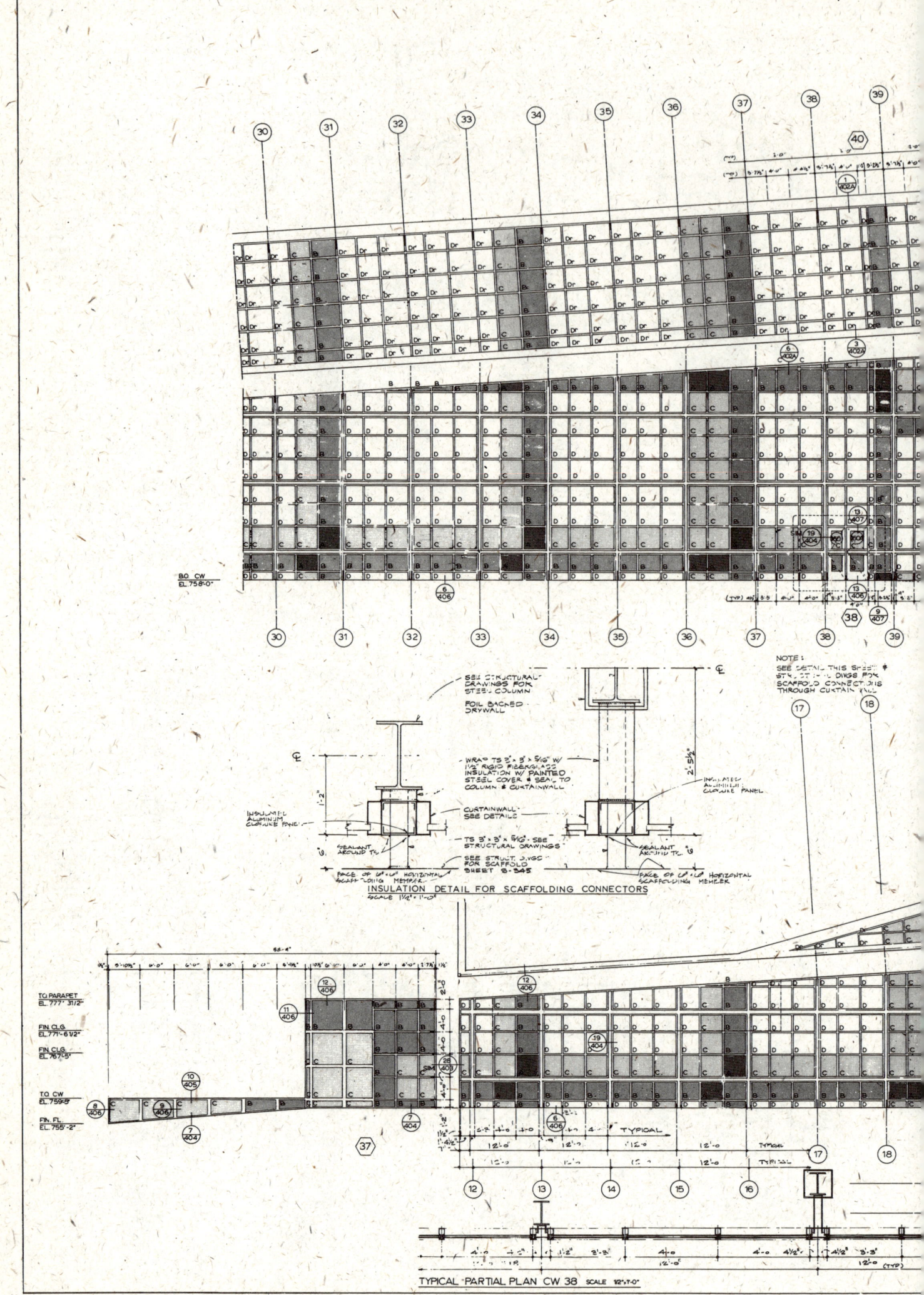

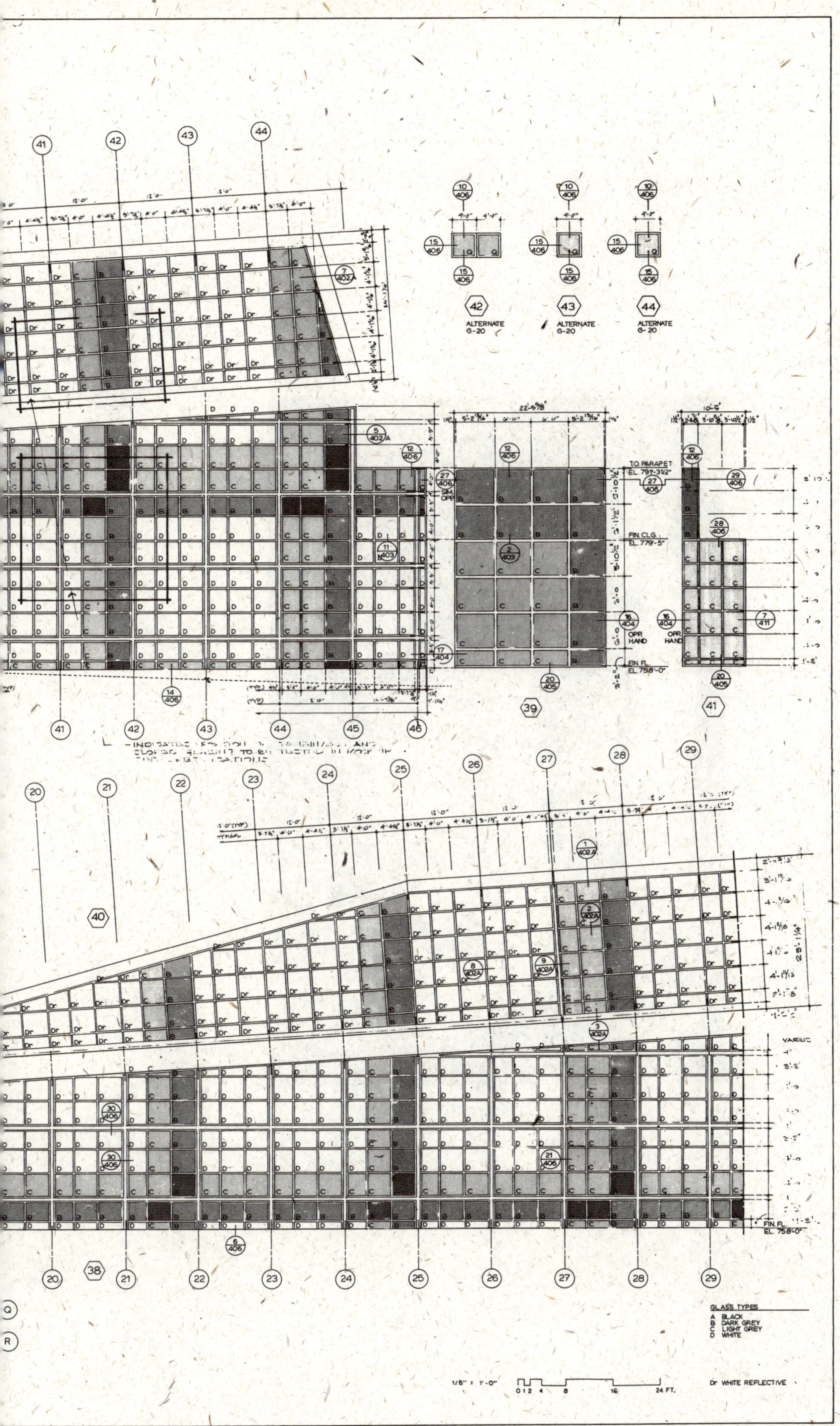

THE OHIO STATE UNIVERSITY

CENTER FOR THE VISUAL ARTS

STATE OF OHIO
DEPARTMENT OF ADMINISTRATIVE SERVICES

DIVISION OF PUBLIC WORKS

TROTT & BEAN/
EISENMAN ROBERTSON
ARCHITECTS, INC.

77E Nationwide Blvd.
Columbus, Ohio 43215
614-221-1469

40 West 25th St.
New York, New York 10010
212-645-1400

HANNA/OLIN, LTD.
Landscape Architects

LANTZ, JONES & NEBRASKA, INC.
Structural Engineers

H.A. WILLIAMS & ASSOCIATES, INC.
Consulting Engineers

State Proj. No.	315 84 190
O.S.U. Proj. No.	A 8213
TB/ER Proj. No.	28140

Drawing Title

WINDOW ELEVATIONS/ SLOPED GLAZING PLAN

Scale: 1/8" = 1'-0" OR AS NOTED

Drawn By: TS, EAC

Checked By:

Drawing No.

A-402

GLASS TYPES
A BLACK
B DARK GREY
C LIGHT GREY
D WHITE
Dr WHITE REFLECTIVE

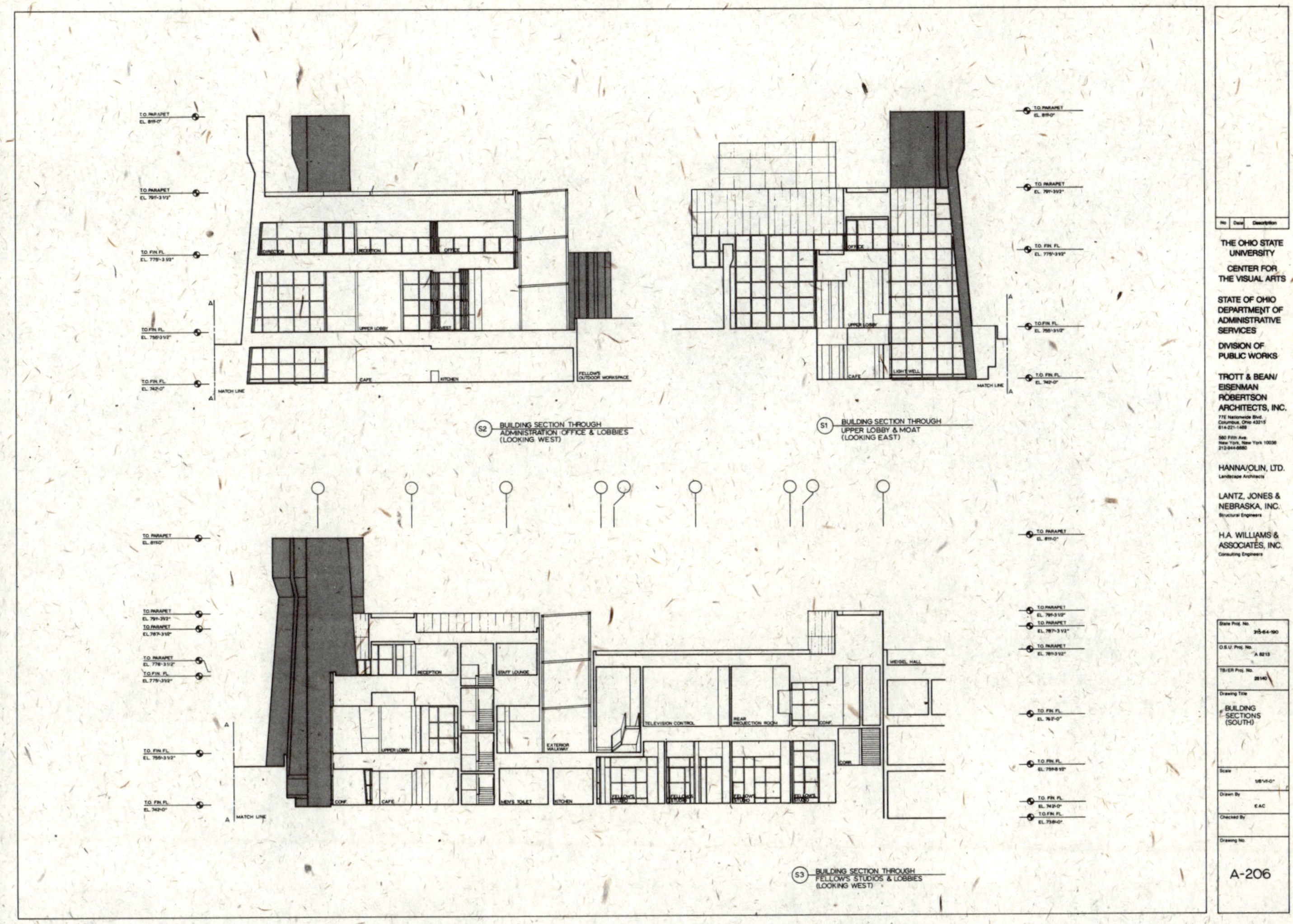

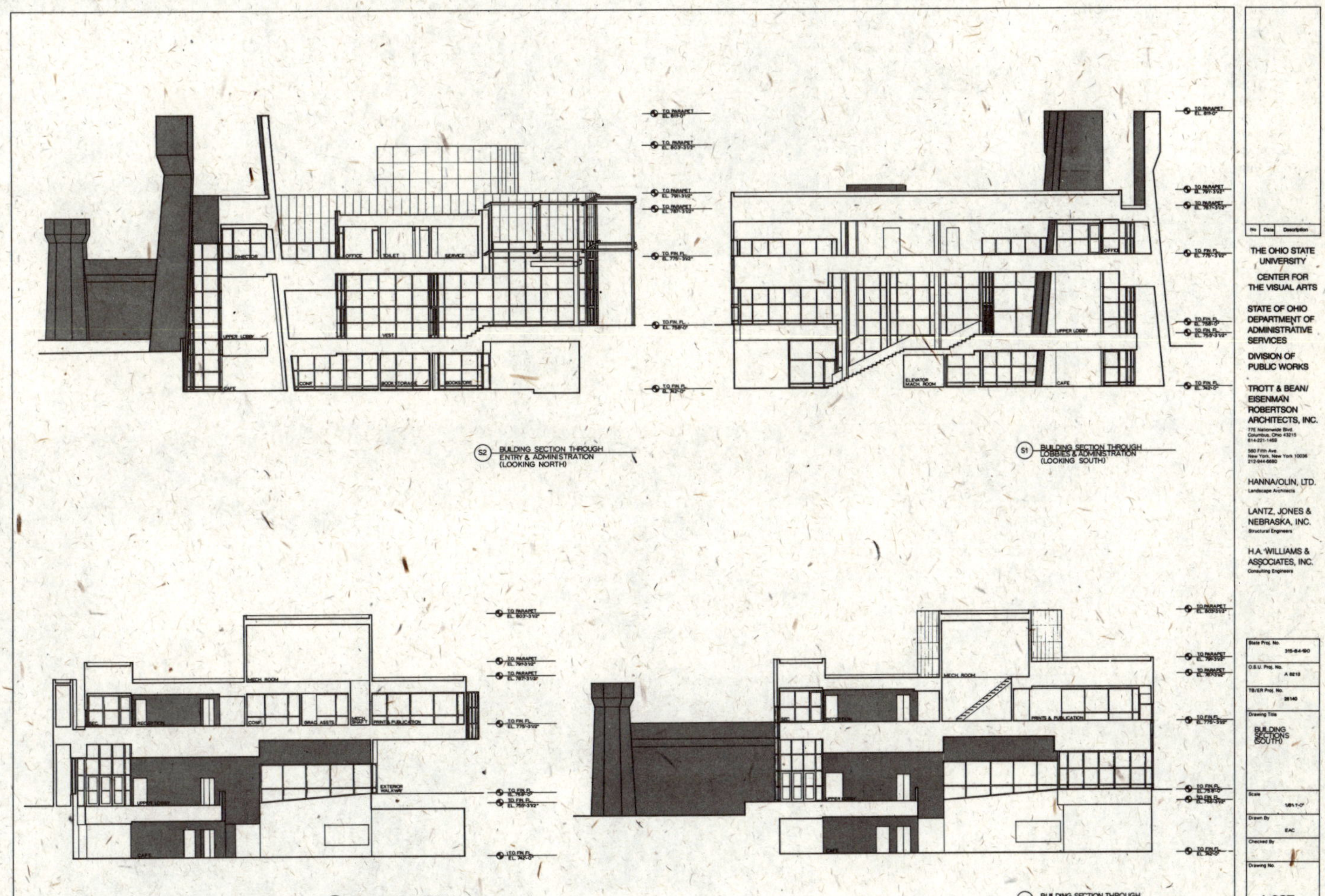

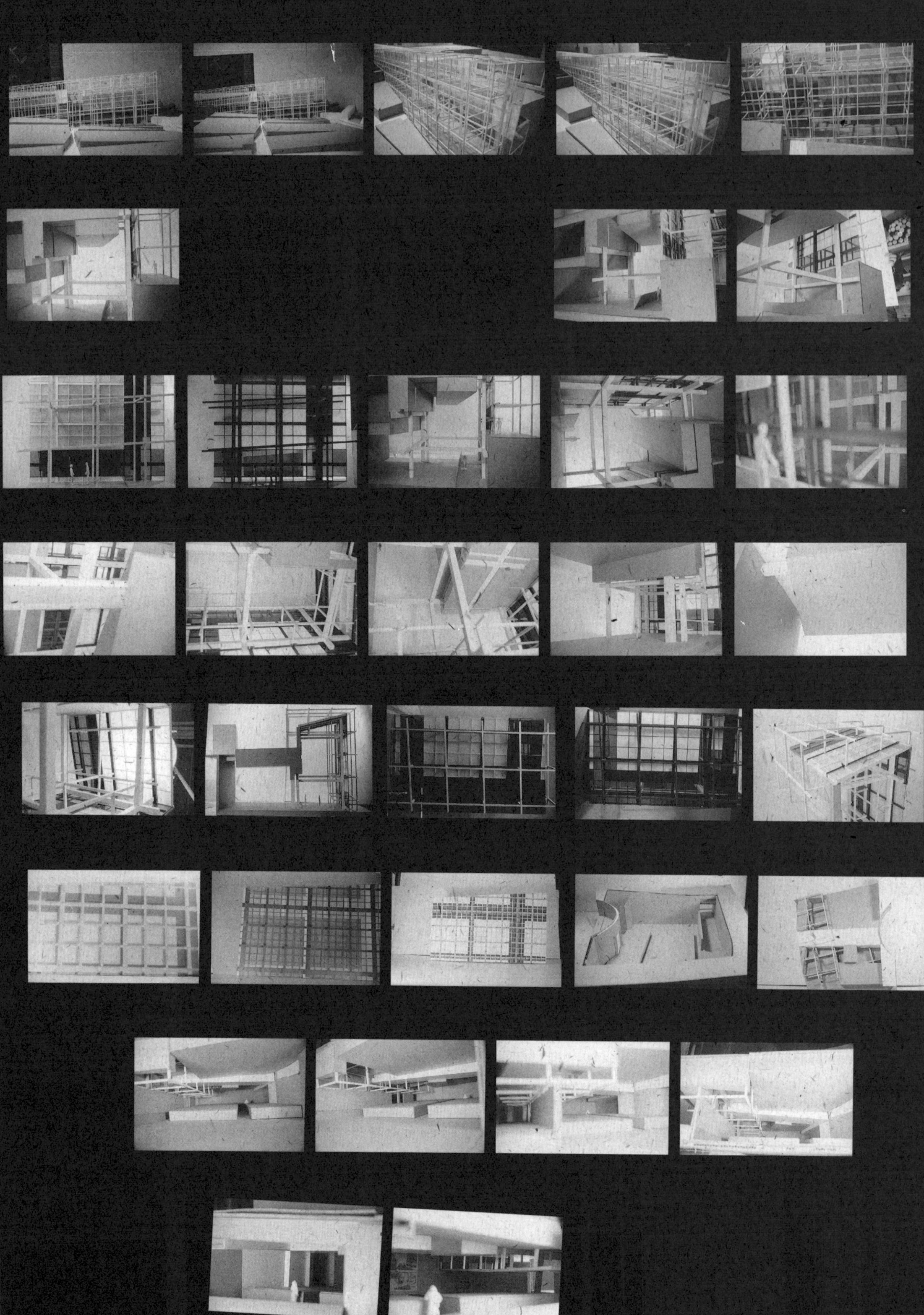

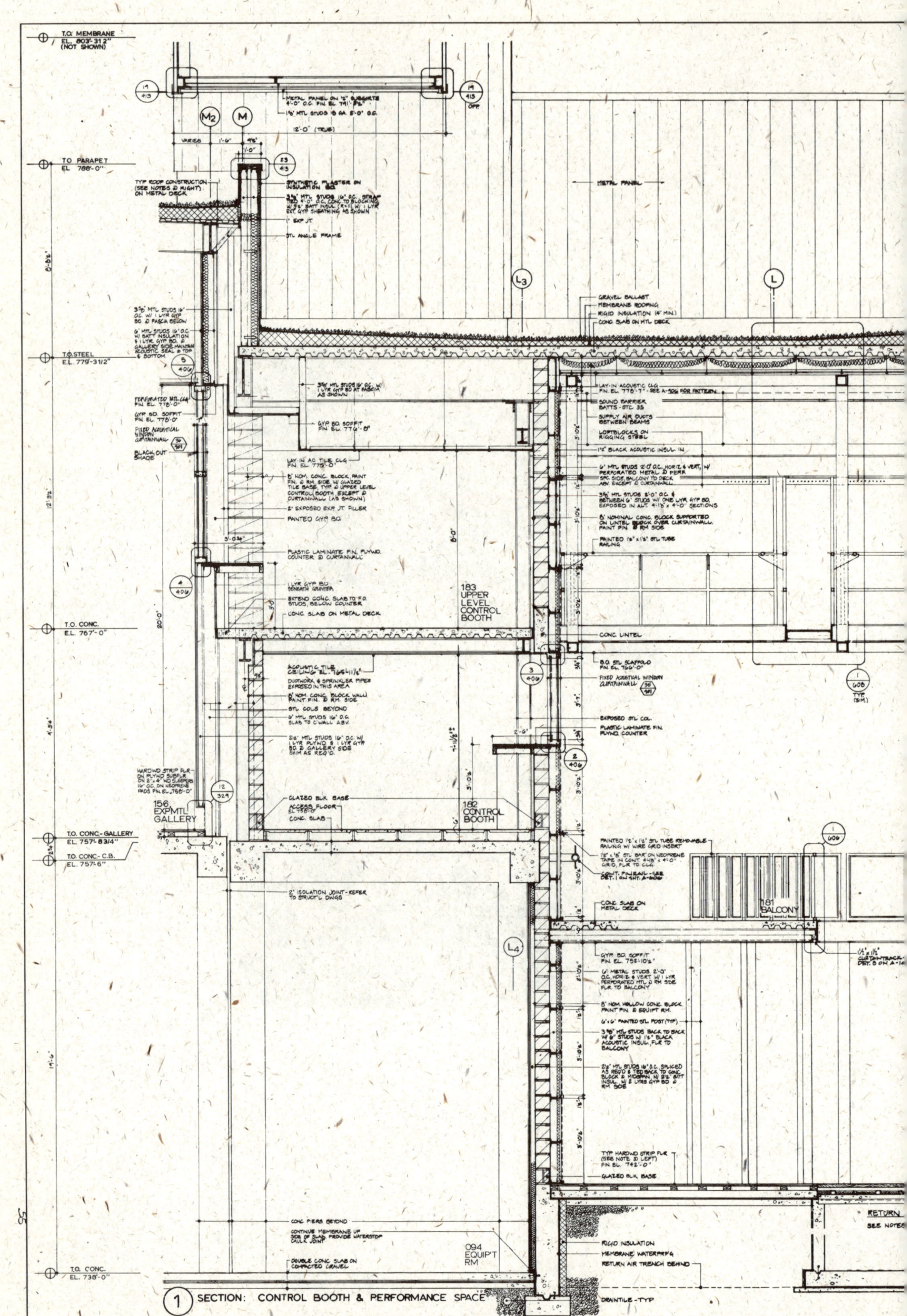

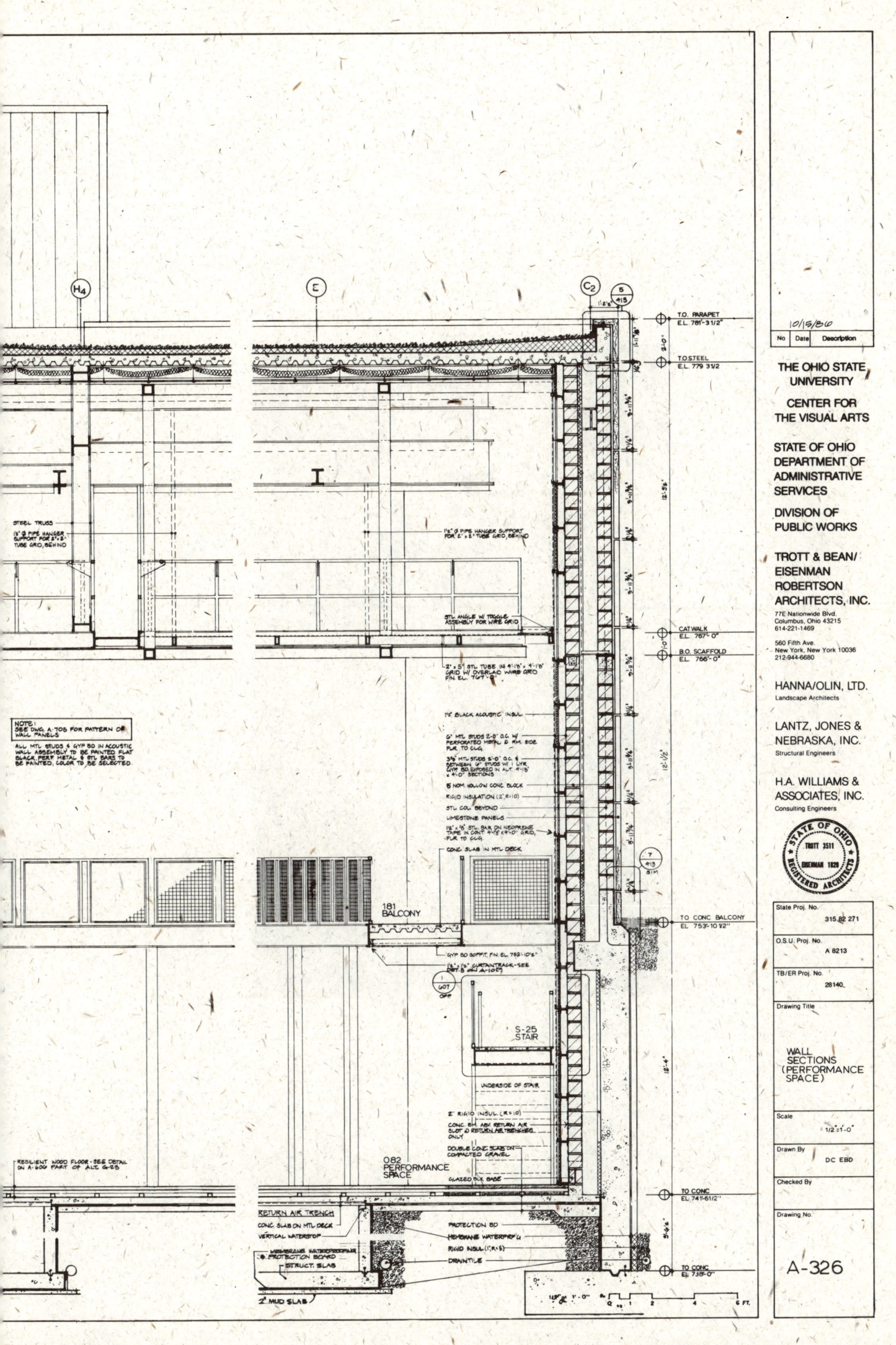

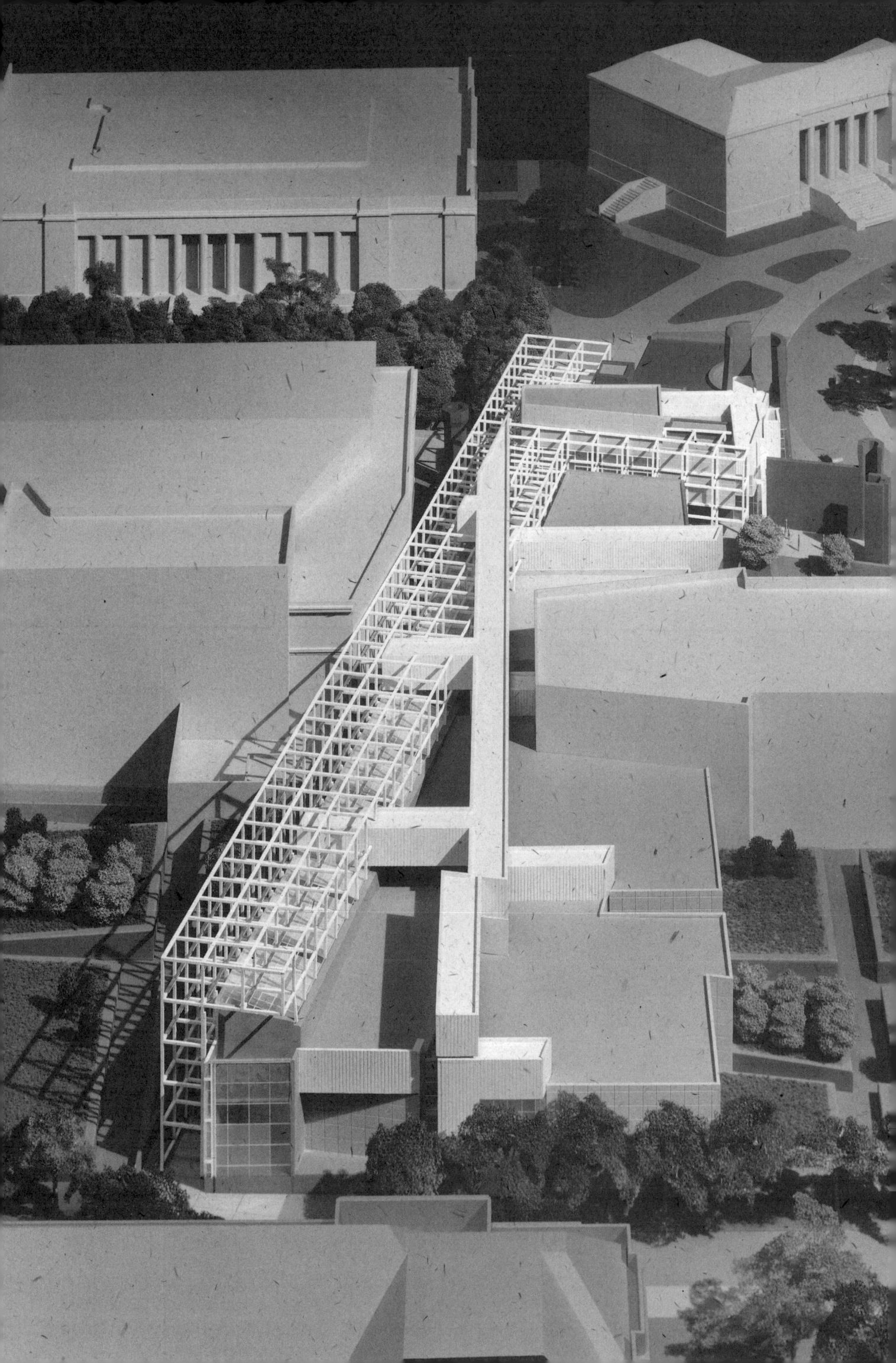

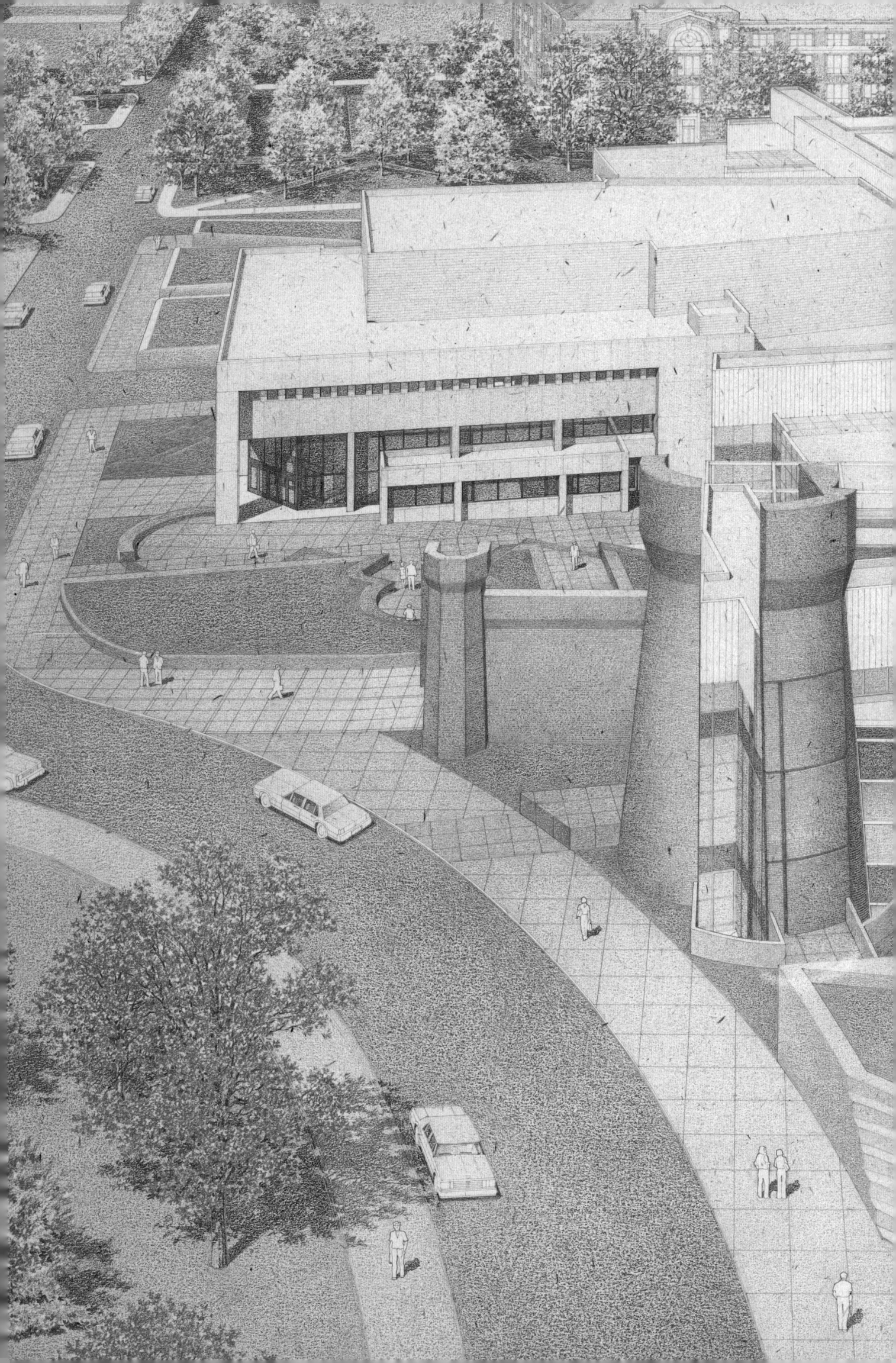

CONSTRUCTION

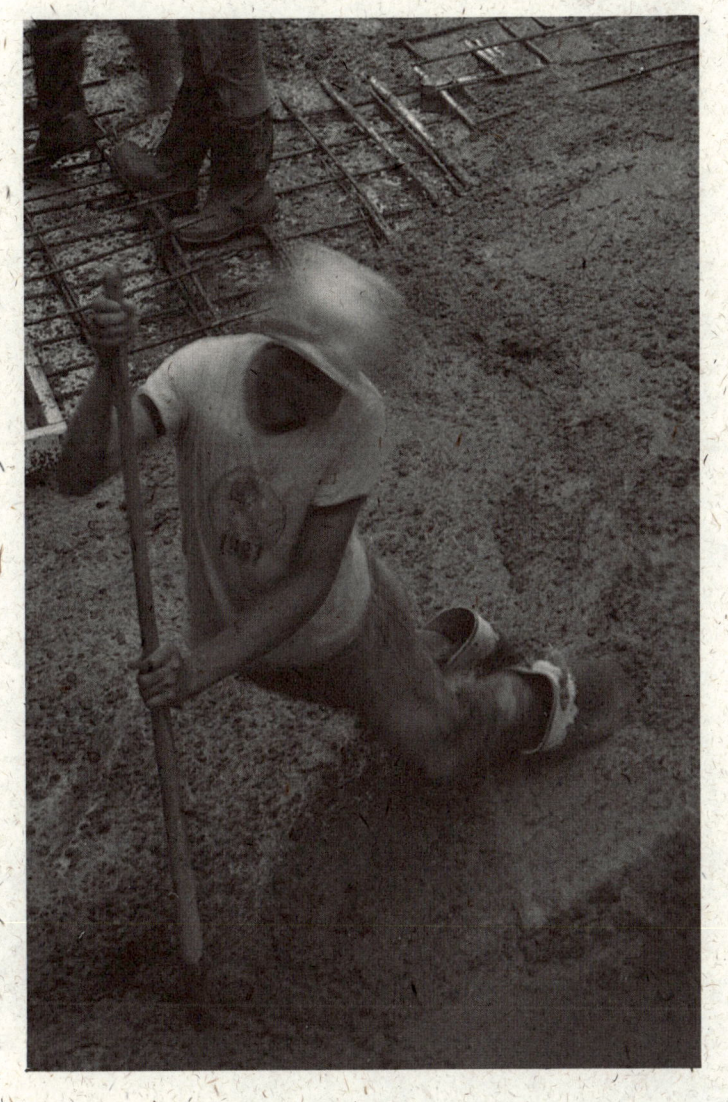

THE BUILDING

THE BUILDING

187